THE PATH TO PERSONAL POWER

Some Other Titles from Falcon Press

Christopher S. Hyatt, Ph.D. & Calvin Iwema
   Energized Hypnosis (book, videos & audios)
Christopher S. Hyatt, Ph.D.
   Undoing Yourself with Energized Meditation and Other Devices
   To Lie Is Human: Not Getting Caught Is Divine
   Secrets of Western Tantra: The Sexuality of the Middle Path
Christopher S. Hyatt, Ph.D. with contributions by
Wm. S. Burroughs, Timothy Leary, Robert Anton Wilson et al.
   Rebels & Devils: The Psychology of Liberation
Christopher S. Hyatt, Ph.D. & Antero Alli
   A Modern Shaman's Guide to a Pregnant Universe
S. Jason Black and Christopher S. Hyatt, Ph.D.
   Pacts with the Devil: A Chronicle of Sex, Blasphemy & Liberation
Antero Alli
   Angel Tech: A Modern Shaman's Guide to Reality Selection
   The Eight-Circuit Brain
Peter J. Carroll
   The Chaos Magick Audios
   PsyberMagick
Phil Hine
   Condensed Chaos: An Introduction to Chaos Magic
   Prime Chaos: Adventures in Chaos Magic
   The Pseudonomicon
Israel Regardie
   The Complete Golden Dawn System of Magic
   New Wings for Daedalus
   The Golden Dawn Audios
Joseph C. Lisiewski, Ph.D.
   Ceremonial Magic and the Power of Evocation
   Kabbalistic Handbook for the Practicing Magician
   Howlings from the Pit
Steven Heller
   Monsters & Magical Sticks: There's No Such Thing as Hypnosis?

For up-to-the-minute information on prices and availability, please visit our website at
http://originalfalcon.com

THE PATH TO PERSONAL POWER

A Guide to Self-Mastery

by
Calvin Iwema, M.A.

THE *Original* FALCON PRESS
TEMPE, ARIZONA, U.S.A.

Copyright © 2021 C.E. by Calvin Iwema

All rights reserved. No part of this book, in part or in whole, may be reproduced, transmitted, or utilized, in any form or by any means, electronic or mechanical, including photocopying, recording, or by any information storage and retrieval system, without permission in writing from the publisher, except for brief quotations in critical articles, books and reviews.

International Standard Book Number: 978-1-935150-69-5
ISBN: 978-1-61869-690-8 (mobi)
ISBN: 978-1-61869-691-5 (ePub)
Library of Congress Control Number: 2021941660

First Edition 2021
First eBook Edition 2021

Front Cover by Jesska Surjik
Cover photograph by Mohamed Almari

Address all inquiries to:
The Original Falcon Press
1753 East Broadway Road #101-277
Tempe, AZ 85282 U.S.A.
(or)
PO Box 3540
Silver Springs NV 89429 U.S.A.
**website: http://www.originalfalcon.com
email: info@originalfalcon.com**

Table of Contents

Introduction 7

Initiation & Attitude

Chapter 1: The Call of More 13
Chapter 2: What Are We Trying to DO Here? 18
Chapter 3: From a Broken Place 26
Chapter 4: So, You Really Want to Take the Red Pill? 29
Chapter 5: Discernment 36
Chapter 6: Learning How to Learn (Again) 39
Chapter 7: Adopting an Effective Learning Stance 42
Chapter 8: Teachers 48

Understanding

Chapter 9: Why Believe in Believing? 53
Chapter 10: Transparency 57
Chapter 11: The Black Box 58
Chapter 12: So, Tell Me About Your Childhood 60
Chapter 13: Opening Your Eyes 69
Chapter 14: Imaginary Problems & Limitations 75
Chapter 15: Picking Up the Pieces 81

The Tipping Point

Chapter 16: Getting Out of Your Own Way 89
Chapter 17: Radical Acceptance 94
Chapter 18: Therapy(ies) 100
Chapter 19: Measuring Progress 103
Chapter 20: What Do You Want? 112

Doing

Chapter 21: From "Knowing Of" to Knowing 117
Chapter 22: DOing 120
Chapter 23: Get Busy—Tips & Tricks for Success 126

Relating

Chapter 24: Playing Well With Others 133
Chapter 25: Relationships & Development 136
Chapter 26: What Is a Healthy Relationship? 140
Chapter 27: The Solitary Path 143
Chapter 28: Elitism & Being Liked 149

Waking Up

Chapter 29: What's Wrong With Just Being? 155
Chapter 30: DIY Enlightenment 158
Chapter 31: You Don't Want This 164
Chapter 32: The Great Paradox 168
Chapter 33: Turning Yourself In 176
Chapter 34: The Overlay 180
Chapter 35: Methods 185
Chapter 36: Cultivation 194
Chapter 37: Dealing With Difficulties 199

Tying It All Together

Chapter 38: Tying It All Together 207
About the Author 214

Introduction

Do you want someone else to be the master of your life? Do you already have plenty of freedom and personal power? Are you just fine with your current level of suffering? Are you happy going through life like a poorly programmed robot? Are you happy serving the agendas of others?

I didn't think so. And, yet, without thinking about these questions, you may unwittingly be living out the answer *yes* to them. By observing the general population, I suspect that not many have asked themselves these questions. Perhaps you are one of the few…

Have you ever wondered why there are so few masters and so many students, and why so few students become masters? This book shows you what it takes to go all the way.

Without pulling any punches *The Path of Personal Power* shows you what attitude is required to walk the path and do the work. Would you like a no-nonsense guide to waking up (shhhh… enlightenment)?

My late mentor and teacher, Dr. Christopher Hyatt, and I shared a personal maxim, which this book helps you put into action:

> **Create your *self* and your life into your own self-styled work of art.**

Many people have an inner inkling that they were destined for *more* yet stop well short of achieving it. They fall prey to the "shoulds" of others and the artificial labels of the polite social majority. This book will jolt you awake so you can avoid these pitfalls and develop the rare quality of being truly self-defining.

The Path synthesizes psychology, philosophy and aspects of Zen to show you how you unknowingly trip yourself up and how to get out of your own way.

The Path provides a balanced approach to mastery, from personal power and working well with others to overcoming your psychological potholes and waking up spiritually.

You will be repeatedly forced to face your human nature. Instead of sheepishly apologizing for it, you will develop the awareness and skills to overcome your human flaws and not be duped by those trying to exploit them. You will become familiar with your neurological development and re-decide some key conclusions you made about yourself and the world you live in, thus increasing your individual freedom and power. Why be a mis-programmed and scared robot when you can become something worthwhile? You will learn to practice *radical acceptance* so, instead of fighting against what has happened in the past, you can stop blaming yourself and get on with your life.

The Path is full of methods for measuring progress and dealing with the difficulties that overcome many who tread the path of personal mastery. You will learn how to be a good student and to take responsibility for your own progress. You will explore how to work effectively with (not *for*) others in your life, from your family and significant others to mentors and society-at-large, without being taken advantage of.

The Path contains the whats, whys and hows that will allow you to achieve escape velocity and **break free from the gravitational pull of the** *average***.**

Great Secret #11
There are no more NOWs that are *not* the right time
to build and live your ideal life.

I would like to thank the following for contributing to my journey:

Dr. Christopher Hyatt
Nick Tharcher
Lauren
Robert Anton Wilson
Timothy Leary
Ken Kesey
Friedrich Nietzsche
Osho
Richard Bandler
Camille Fraga Jones

Calvin Iwema

Margie Salyer
Gary Weber
Carlos Castaneda
All of my clients

Initiation & Attitude

Chapter 1
The Call of *More*

It was late afternoon on a hot and sunny summer day when I heard my mother attempt to choke out my name for help. As I struggled to see inside the dark house through the screen door, I could just make out my father's hands wrapped around her neck and see her squirming to break free. She managed to get loose and I remember I was so scared that I couldn't move or speak. As I walked away down the driveway in shock, I recall the feelings of anger and annoyance that she asked me for my help at all. I'm not sure what she thought a 12-year-old would be able to do, but I was relieved that my father was either drunk enough or smart enough to let her go and I didn't have to see her dead on the floor, forcing me to live out my days with my father.

It was one of those moments one has when something inside *clicks* and a truth is realized that cannot be unlearned. As my heart and mind raced, a deep inner *knowing* emerged from behind my fear and anxiety. Something was up around here!! It was a true loss of innocence, and if life was letting me down, then I wasn't going to play along and go quietly. Out of this sense of loss arose a clear understanding that there had to be more to be gained from life than what I was currently experiencing. It was also clear that if it was possible for life to be better, it wasn't those two in the house that were going to bring it about.

At that moment I promised myself that I would go to any lengths to figure life out. I would rather die trying than be destined to follow in the footsteps of those around me—playing a pointless game while pretending that they were doing something noble.

It was at that moment that I became a seeker. What was I seeking? *More.* At that point I knew there had to be *More* out there for me somewhere.

From a young age it was apparent to me through simple observation that other people were doing different things and getting better results in life. They had nice things, a clean home and well-cared-for yard. They went on vacations and seemed to enjoy learning. They didn't yell at each other or beat each other, pass out drunk and then pretend that all was normal.

Through these comparisons against others around me I couldn't see a valid reason for living the way we did. I couldn't imagine why one would build this kind of life around themselves. So, I *asked*. There were stories (excuses), personal values (fear), and the simple repetition of "it's always been done that way" (history). If that wasn't enough, there was always religion (superstition and obedience) which confused me since those rules were either outright ignored or twisted to serve the whim or tantrum of the moment. The last-ditch answer was a version of "drop it/because I say so" that was enforced through psychological violence and, if need be, physical violence. Yet none of these justifications could outshine the blinding truth: there were no good results coming from this lifestyle and belief system. It just didn't work out very well if measured in an objective, pragmatic way.

The only way you can make sense of what I have described and to "win" at that version of the game of life is to give yourself imaginary points for serving your own narcissism and insecurity and labeling your inherent suffering and failure as virtues. In this way, you can collect points for allegiance to self-serving concepts and defend the corresponding behaviors regardless of the negative impact and (lack of) results.

Playing along with this lose-lose existence while pretending I was benefitting from it in some way was not an option for me as I pictured myself as an adult—I wanted to win for real. The basic truth that I discovered that hot summer day long ago has been confirmed over and over again through the years by the people I have known, observed, studied under and worked with. It is a truth that is easier to see than to admit, and it haunts people while it hides in plain sight:

> The cost of the average, mediocre and unenlightened life is greater than its reward…
> and therefore not worth living.

The Path to Personal Power

This realization scared me more than it inspired me at first. I saw firsthand the downside of not pursuing **More**. I knew that if I didn't do what it takes, whatever that would be, I would be screwed and end up with **Less** *and perhaps with* **Nothing.**

I was scared because I wasn't sure if *I* could win. I knew that I did not want to be a failure and a living monument to mediocrity. I did not want to suffer for the rest of my life like those around me. I especially did not want to work for decades to find myself in a desperate place like my father—working towards losing everything he loved, unable to get out of his own way.

Alongside my fear I also had an inner inkling—a sense that seemed to come both from within and beyond me—to pursue **More**. So that day I promised myself that I would do my very best to pursue **More** for myself as I went through life. In no way was I sure I could do it, follow through with it or if anything good would ever come my way from it. And despite my fear, that inner sense seemed to be *enough.* And at the end of that hot summer day, it seemed it was all I had.

Now look deeper. What specifically was "all I had"? What I had was the *decision.* The inkling that there is **More** out there for you is what I refer to as the **Call**. It is analogous to an animal out in the woods calling out to another. It is **your decision** to either say yes or no to it. It is your call to learn, grow, expand, create and love. It is your call to say **Yes** both to life and to yourself. The call was *enough* in that moment to get me through that experience and set a direction to focus on. Difficult experiences like the one I shared are actually a great gift because they have the power to wake you up. They are invaluable because they can trigger the awareness that a decision to be made *even exists.* It is good practice to keep these experiences close to you, not as an excuse to feel sorry for yourself or set low standards, but for strengthening your connection to your own call.

At first the call is faint, and to succeed on the path to self-mastery you have to strengthen your connection to it. This is done by being open to it and creating space and silence for it. To create space, you will have to get your ego to quit hogging the spotlight with its drama and false promises. In other words, you have to learn how to get out of your own way. Strengthening your connection to the call will build your drive, commitment and resolve to do the tough work necessary.

The concept of *More* arises out of comparison. Look at your life. You are constantly exposed to excellence, greatness and all types of creativity. You can easily find many examples of overcoming, success, and if you look closely enough, mastery itself. You are constantly comparing yourself, your results and your lot in life to others. At some level you already know this. You already know there is a gap between where you are and what you want for yourself—unless you are completely asleep at the wheel. You know it because you see the differences between yourself and others. You know it because you can imagine a better version of yourself and your life.

> The *call* is your inner inkling to do something about that difference.

For some the call comes at a point in their life when they are exposed to an inspiration and an important choice—whether or not to follow the opportunity that *More* presents. It is a common theme demonstrated in the archetypal hero's journey told to us in stories like *Star Wars* and *The Matrix*. Consider the following scene from the television pilot of *Kung Fu*.

> *A young boy waits with others outside the Shaolin temple hoping to gain admittance to live and study. After a time, some are admitted while he and others are told to go home. Some of the boys play, while a few stand by the door patiently and quietly out of respect. Those who were playing are sent home. A few more are admitted and the rest are told that there is no hope for them and to return to their homes. When the thunder comes, followed by the wind and driving rain, many boys scatter to find shelter while one stands dutifully, staring at the door and braving the elements. After much perseverance and through showing great respect he is finally admitted and allowed to study and live within the temple.*

What inspires the boy to show up? Why sit in the rain—let alone endure all the hardships that will come from this training? What inspires *anyone* to journey down an esoteric path of personal development? The boy shows up because of the *promise* of more. He wants

The Path to Personal Power

things for himself and his life that he does not yet have. He sees opportunities to live life in a better way with the rewards that entails.

The call of more begs your decision. The young boy finds determination and persistence through having said "yes" to the call. It is a commitment to himself. The commitment to himself is his *why*.

> The commitment to yourself is your strongest WHY.

The commitment to yourself is your strongest *why*. If you are having trouble saying "yes" to more, then you need to ask yourself why you don't value and honor yourself enough. To answer the call of more is to commit to more of *you*.

Closely connected to the decision to pursue more is the search for *how* to get more. To search for *how* is to search for *the path*. In the case of the young boy, the path he chose was the Shaolin Temple. Being exposed to those monks may have also triggered his call to more. Sometimes the *how,* when presented to us, is the comparison that shows us there is more to us and for us; it starts the ball rolling. The young boy is certain that within those walls are the methods and techniques—*the path*—to mastery of himself and his environment—and if he's so inclined—answers to the mysteries of life.

The term *path* is often seen in spiritual and occult literature. For our purposes we will define it as a philosophy and methodology for learning and unlearning what we really are as we pursue *more*.

> ~ EXERCISE ~
> How are you going to answer the call?
> What are you going to do about it?
> Are you fully committed to your true self?

Chapter 2
What Are We Trying to DO Here?

Esoteric literature is full of terms like *the path, the great work* and even (gasp) *enlightenment*. Also found are themes of becoming, increasing personal power and learning how to make your external reality conform to your wishes. These imply a purpose and/or an end goal. I'm not sure what statement of purpose you may be expecting, and it's a question worth exploring.

So… What are we trying to do here??

> The overall goal is to discover what you really are by acquiring personal power and developing self-mastery.

The idea of self-mastery implies a lot. Continual learning and growth leading to the acquisition of skill and discipline are certainly primary. As are having a personal philosophy, character and integrity. Having your psychological house in order—which includes not letting emotions get the best of you while accepting them and utilizing them. Understanding your nervous system instead of being victimized by it and developing a reasonably thick skin.

Self-mastery and personal power have a *yin* and *yang* relationship. Self-mastery includes the acquisition of personal power which is directed at DOing more in life. Doing and accomplishing things in life creates free time and space to go inside and explore your own BEing. Self-mastery also includes looking inward and DOing.

My definition of personal power is the *ability* to achieve a personalized, desired result. Increasing your level of personal power brings *more* of what enhances your experience of life and *less* of what diminishes it. *More* strength, results, understanding, satisfaction and joy; and *less* weakness, fear, suffering, ignorance and anxiety. These attributes of power enable you to tip the scales in your favor when opportunities arise and critical decisions must be made. The converse is also true: not having enough power and its attributes will contribute to your coming up short. Opportunities are lost due to a lack of resources, mishandled due to a lack of maturity or temperance, or not seen in the first place due to a lack of perspective and awareness. Thus, it is fair to say that we pursue power simply to have more direct influence and control over the course and outcomes of our lives.

The ideal I am describing through self-mastery and personal power is beyond the rudimentary drive for self-improvement that most people fulfill through education, career advancement, more and "better" partners, pop-psychology, and surface-level religion. What we are looking at, and what is often so subtle, goes deeper than surface-level to the deliberate intent and action to know what we truly are. The inspiration and motivation required to reach this understanding are more than the basic drive to "feel better," although the journey often starts with just that.

There is a perspective that sees personal power as a *means to an end*, that I call the *DOing* perspective. It is quite obvious (to some; as Voltaire said, "Common sense is not so common") that this can be a vast improvement over ordinary life. The DOing aspects of power include skill development, strength, health, education, resources, relationship skills, and communication.

There is another, more subtle and yet equally important perspective of power that needs to be included—the *Understanding* side. Its aspects include knowledge, discernment and wisdom, all of which are necessary for self-mastery.

Thoreau alludes to both aspects of power and captures the overall goal of self-mastery elegantly in his summary to *Walden*:

> *I learned this, at least, by my experiment: that if one advances confidently in the direction of his dreams, and endeavors to live the life which he has imagined; he will meet with a success unexpected in common hours. He will put some things behind, will pass an invisible boundary...and he will live with the license of a higher order of beings.*

To live with the license of a higher order of beings implies something beyond the common, materialistic *DOing* definition of success (not that there is anything wrong with that…in fact, we *encourage* it). Thoreau hints at a spiritual component, and the realm of *masters*—the elevation of human experience far beyond its "normal" baseline. The *understanding* perspective not only sweetens the normal measures of success, but highlights power as an *end in-an-of-itself*. This culminates in the knowledge and experience of what you truly are.

> **Knowing and DOing are often portrayed as a paradox. We prefer to solve paradoxes rather than be fooled by them.**

Paradoxes tend to be unnecessary distractions and can lead to long dead ends. One of my least favorite distractions is the argument of spiritual and material goals. One way to illustrate this and uncover any underlying bias you may have (been taught) is through the following:

> **~ EXERCISE ~**
> Read through the following list. Note if you are drawn to one of the pairs more than the other, or if one seems "bad" or "wrong." Note the ones you are most drawn to or feel "right" for you.
> Be honest with yourself. There are no right or wrong answers.

Self-Mastery	Personal Power
Spiritual	Material/Physical
Eastern	Western
Sublime	Mundane
Being	Having
Right Hand Path	Left Hand Path
Inner	Outer
Religious	Scientific
Belief	Proof/Data
Enlightenment	Success/Wealth
Wave	Particle
Knowing	Doing
Understanding	Accomplishing

> Why didn't you mark all of them?
> Are you trying to short-change yourself?

The categories make up two worlds, and *self-mastery* and *personal power* do not necessarily serve as accurate categories for the word pairs. The point is that false dichotomies and dualistic thinking are almost always preset in society and organized religion. We refer to people with a vested interest in one belief system as "true believers," a term coined by Eric Hoffer in his book *The True Believer: Thoughts on the Nature of Mass Movements*. True believers are mostly fanatical and extreme, and their emotionality far eclipses rational thought and openness to new ideas (and facts).

True believers are easily controlled to pursue ends that are not their own. The need for identity, belonging and validation are more important than their own truth, integrity and personal development.

Proponents (True Believers) of spiritual pursuits value the spiritual and metaphysical over the materialistic and physical. They often look down upon the physical and mundane as if they are unnatural, dirty and evil. Often this is the case because they prefer their inner fantasy and earning spiritual "points" instead of hard work that challenges their ego. They forego the physical and material pleasures of life because they feel guilty and/or undeserving of them. But there is nothing noble about not bathing, living in a hovel and having holes in your shoes.

On the other hand, proponents of materialistic and physical pursuits (True Believers) value these over the spiritual and metaphysical. They would rather increase their physical power, wealth, skill and status than be "holy." They can, at times, tend to have frighteningly low self-awareness and appear to have little likelihood of waking up. They do, however, enjoy the fruits of physical power and material success. Still there is nothing noble about having a pile of money, being asleep at the wheel and suffering the same ordinary psychological plights as everyone else. (This is not a statement against money...it is just that having money or status cannot bypass or substitute for the results of inner work.)

"Spiritual" types often parrot the *absolute perspective* of sages, reminding us that there is "no true nature that can be broken," nothing can be added or improved in terms of our real self and true nature. (Let alone horseshit like, "If god wanted us to fly, he'd have given us wings.") While these perspectives will come into light at later parts of the journey, they are usually just repeated by those *without direct experience* of them. If you are honest with yourself, it is hard to argue the here-and-now *relative perspective* where more power, wealth, skill and accomplishment are "better" than less.

The above perspectives and statements are from the extreme ends of a continuum. While looking at the word-pair list you might have noticed that they represent a sampling of unnecessary dichotomies and dualisms that are present in just about every discussion, book or belief system (including religion) involving "spiritual" development. These are often nothing more than *beliefs* that people hide behind and that need to be challenged.

The proponents of one aspect tend to vilify the other aspect, and in that false division bind themselves to imbalance and missing the big picture. The opposing aspects exist only in language and concept, as no one thing can be separated out of the *one whole everything* anyway.

The argument for spiritual vs. material and knowing vs. doing has worn out its welcome. It is a great example of the purpose (accidental or nefarious) of philosophical and political dualism—to keep people enslaved by their human nature. The human nature I refer to is the untrained and lazy mind that is enslaved by the inability to discern the conceptual from the real. Two things to consider: the spiritual journey isn't made up of opposites, and True Believers never synthesize the opposites. Instead, one side overcomes the other by force. People like to give themselves "identities" and "bonus points" for following a pre-prescribed belief system while hurling insults and judgment at the other side. Because of this charade, *adherence to a belief system* is much more important to a true believer than ***actual results.***

> Why not ***get real results in life*** instead of collecting imaginary points in a game that was designed to keep you in the dark?

You can choose to focus solely on one aspect if you'd like—either "regular life" or "spiritual development." Just keep in mind that this decision is based on a belief system that sees playing small as a virtue.

The Path to Personal Power

The primary reason for pursuing *both* sides is that you will get more *real results*. You will progress much faster and with less suffering. The paths to spiritual/psychological development and to success, for example, act as a multiplier for each other. You learn more about your fears when you interface with the real world than you do by contemplating them on your sofa. The real world is also the best (and *only*) testing ground for your progress in *applying* what you learn about yourself and your true nature. The real world is the best teacher of lessons, where you *apply what you know* (or think you know). This will often show you your true level of progress, and where you still need to work.

> **You can look at the work as two worlds. In that case, you should have a foot in each.**

Working on the mundane creates power and momentum for the sublime. Advancing your education, career and relationships, for example, gives you both confidence and the opportunity to apply and test your spiritual work. In this case the mundane produces confidence and security, freeing up focus and energy to be applied in the sublime. Working on the sublime refines self-knowledge, hones insight, and provides peace and healing. This reduces fear and creates true understanding, freeing up attention and energy to be applied in the mundane. The resulting upward spiral propels one forward and becomes more and more self-sustaining.

I'd like you to ponder the following sentence long and hard, because I think it is extremely important:

> **On one hand a student on the path of personal power seeks to "wake up" in a profound spiritual sense, and on the other hand he will wake up into the same life he *already has*.**

Why not make that entire life—the one you will wake up in—outstanding? There is an old saying: *"Before enlightenment, chop wood and carry water. After enlightenment, chop wood and carry water."* Don't you think it's possible that the originator of this idea may have intended the phrase *chop wood and carry water* as a metaphor for your ***entire life***?

You might also start to consider that the "waking up" we are looking into means more than smiling at others and lighting incense. If we are looking at taking the idea of waking up all the way, then we are working towards Zen enlightenment.

> **HOLY SHIT ALERT**
> The author just used the word "enlightenment"!

The spiritual end goal and crowning achievement is often labeled as *enlightenment*. I've always found it interesting that this subject is seldom addressed in occult literature. This goal has been so poorly misrepresented and buried beneath language and cultural barriers, myth, religious dogma and pop-culture, that two things have happened. One is that most have abandoned the search altogether, and the other is that the topic has become taboo. It has been relegated to the flakes, the totally misguided (those who will believe in anything), and those who have no inclination towards personal power. This is unfortunate, and this topic will be explored head-on in this book.

Some will say that power is bad…and that it should not be pursued. These are people who have made weakness a virtue and worship it. They hang out with other weak people. They have forgotten how to win, and they believe that winning isn't all that great anyway. They secretly want to dominate you…in a passive-aggressive way, of course. Saying that power is bad because it can be abused is another way to bolster their weakness. This is like saying a hammer is bad because it can be abused.

Let's admit our true nature and embrace our human-ness. Attempting to split off and disown parts of yourself—your foibles, shortcomings and failures—won't help nor will it work. If you look at your hang-ups, you will likely find that these are areas where your power was taken from you (by rules, parents, society and belief systems). In other words, this is where you *gave away* your power.

Maybe you should take your power back. It is not becoming of power to be apologetic about power itself or your deliberate pursuit of it. It is not becoming of your true self and its full potential to be apologetic at all. Remember our definition of personal power: *the ability to achieve a personalized, desired result*. This in no way implies a license to be an asshole and violently storm through the world, taking and doing whatever you want no matter the cost. The view that paints power as evil is simple propaganda and brainwashing perpetrated by those who have refused to *think* and those with little power other than what is provided through belonging to a *True Believer* group. They are afraid, and they are afraid of your power. They are unconsciously self-loathing, and your real-world results become the mirror that shows them what they are and what they have not accomplished. (You might refer to Christopher Hyatt's *The Psychopath's Bible,* Falcon Press for further discussion.) Despite occasionally disturbing others and hurting their feelings, I still refuse to apologize. I refuse because I know that the mirror also reminds them of what they *could be* and this is a gift (although painful) in the fact that it may prove to be their wake-up *call.*

~ EXERCISE ~
Where in life, for the benefit of others, do you live apologetically, hide your power and edit your preferences?

My late teacher, Dr. Christopher Hyatt, was fond of the directive **"Make yourself and your life into a self-styled work of art."** I have included an important component to the end of this statement, which is not my invention, but my experience in working with him. Although you may not have read it before, it sheds light on both the nature of this path and Hyatt himself.

Make yourself and your life into a work of art...
while working on waking up.

Walk through life with a foot in each world...unapologetically.

~ EXERCISE ~
What does You and Your Life as a work of art look like?

Chapter 3
From a Broken Place

In the last chapter, we looked at the goal of "Making yourself into a work of art while you work on waking up." This can seem quite a lofty goal if you are in a lot of pain and oftentimes don't like yourself very much or believe in yourself enough.

I think it makes sense to talk plainly about this up front. Along with many of the people with whom I have worked, you may be coming to these ideas from what you might call "a broken place." They have had a tough go in life. Most have had difficult and painful childhoods, often without enough truth and preparation for life. This can easily result in all kinds of psychological maladies—the least of which are self-imposed limitations, doubts, fears and guilt. Untreated, this will often lead to unnecessary suffering and missed opportunities. It is quite common to see people struggling to transition to adulthood and take responsibility for their lives, and there are plenty of failed educations, careers and relationships evident as proof. Childhood development doesn't need to include intentional harm in order to go awry. (We will explore this more later.) Few people come out of their early development unscathed, fully self-aware and ready for life. So, with that said…

> No matter where you are starting from, or what condition you find yourself in, **YOU** are responsible for the totality of your entire life.

The idea that you are responsible for the totality of your life often comes as a shock to people because they have never stopped to think about it. Are you expecting someone else to do it for you? Are you leaving important aspects of your life to chance? (Now is a good time to stop and think about it.) From my experience, it seems to be an especially difficult pill to swallow for people who have had a difficult past.

The Path to Personal Power

The summer before high school I ran into some trouble with the law. While I was at the lowest of my lows and feeling hopeless and desperate, I came across the following quote...

> If it's going to be, it's up to **me**.

From the moment I read it I knew it was a fact I could not escape. I also took it to mean that while other people couldn't do my success for me, they also couldn't talk me out of it or screw it up either. The outcomes of those around me (or lack of outcomes) did not predict my own future. Having my entire life in my own hands was scary and also the best hands to have them in.

Not long after my realization I shared the quote and my fears around it to my therapist. This caused our session to take an immediate deep dive, much different than our previous visits. The conversation turned to me taking responsibility for my life. I was resistant to this idea out of fear, and quickly pulled out the long list of things that had been done to me and that I had not been given. He told me that I was using my list of wrongs as a reason for not taking responsibility and, while that was understandable as a part of grieving, it wasn't going to get me what I wanted out of life as a long-term strategy.

I had never been presented with anything like this before. I could not put any words together. I remember just staring at him feeling a combination of sadness, fear and anger. He continued on by teaching me that responsibility was a good thing. He said that the word responsibility could be spelled response-ability, meaning that I was able to choose how I respond to life. That instead of "having to" be responsible I "get to" choose how I respond to life. "Having to" makes life a chore while "getting to" makes it an adventure. Where I currently found myself in my life at that time—my situation—may or may not have been my fault, but it was up to me to move forward. I was responsible for the decision and had freedom in that process.

We came up with a lot of examples that were fun and empowering. Despite having had some bad times and weird experiences, I could get good grades. Instead of pouting about my situation, I started buying my own clothes with my paper route money and developed my own sense of style. We found metaphorical lemons and turned them into lemonade. I learned through my own efforts that being a "lemonade-maker" gave me personal power and self-efficacy. I learned that I could come to choice on being a victim or overcomer, and that this was a choice that was within my control.

Coming from a broken place or not, there will be times when you feel hurt, down and full of self-pity. You will be afraid and lack confidence. It will seem that you have to take extra steps just to get to *neutral*, just to get to "normal," and this may be true. Once you have gotten back to normal then there is more work to come on the way to becoming outstanding. You will need to take extra steps to catch up to those people who haven't had it as tough as you have. You will need to come to terms with this and decide to do the work anyway.

You can find some solace in the fact that *nobody is "normal"*—everyone has different strengths, weaknesses, advantages and disadvantages. You will do more work than others, and some will need to do more than you in one area or another.

In much of life you cannot control what cards you are dealt. You *can* come to choice at how you play them.

The best revenge is success, and that success is going to take what it is going to take.

> **~ EXERCISE ~**
> I challenge you to accept yourself, your current life and your past...*AS THEY ARE.*
> Then I want you to commit to moving forward, regardless of what it takes to create yourself and your life into a work of art.

Consider the following quote:

> "It is not enough that we do our best; sometimes we must do what is required."
> — Winston Churchill

If you commit to this, you can achieve what you want. If you chose to "give it your best shot" then you can expect to fall short at some point. Doing what is required does not change because of your past or your story. If you choose not to accept responsibility for the totality of your life, either someone else will or you are leaving it up to chance.

Chapter 4
So, You Really Want to Take the Red Pill?

Many people have heard the Call of More and are *seeking*.

One thing that this broad audience has in common is that they are quite often drawn to the archetype of *the Master*. Examples include Obi Wan Kenobi and Yoda from *Star Wars,* and Morpheus in *The Matrix*. We are mesmerized by these *Masters* who often possess (and flaunt) some combination of super-human skills, abilities, wisdom and riches. I would bet that most of this audience would state with certainty that if they were ever offered the opportunity, they would without a doubt take the *red pill*. (In the movie *The Matrix* the master offers the student a choice: swallowing the red pill, the student will see his true reality, a choice which he cannot undo; if he chooses the blue pill, he can forever stay in regular life and forget about the choice. The term "red-pilled" has been borrowed by some social movements; please ignore them.)

Swallowing the red pill is a metaphor for initiation.

Initiation is a commitment and a promise. Mostly to yourself and somewhat to the methods and those that teach them. The idea of initiation is to ready yourself for what is ahead.

The fantasies we have about the path and our internal montage about doing the work are fun. At some level they give us meaning, purpose and identity, especially in the early stages. Winning imaginary games is an ego boost. As you commit to yourself and this path and do the work, you will begin to understand firsthand what is hard, what is necessary and what *works*. You will also learn what is a waste of time and produces no results other than ego-boosts and inflated self-labels. You will learn what it really takes to succeed and achieve. These learnings cannot be unlearned, and what has been seen cannot be unseen. The gap between how we *think* it is going to be, and what it really takes, is painful and frustrating. It is a direct affront to the fragile ego.

These gaps between what we have been told, sold and "believe" and what really produces next-level results come up from time to time. At this point there are two choices. The first is to disregard the new information and stick to the beliefs and labels. This keeps you play-acting and pretending to be doing something worthwhile. The occult (indeed the world) is full of people who have cut their journey short in this manner. These people are happy with just the label, the membership card and the identity they think comes from these. *But putting on a Superman costume does not give you super-powers.*

The second choice is to come to terms with the new information and higher standards, accept them and the extra effort required, and push on. Those who make this decision are choosing for their power and results over their ego.

Those who decide to not push on are fooling themselves, and this will forever limit them. There is a cost to *knowing-better and not-doing*. This decision is saying *no* to reality and *no* to oneself. It is a breach of integrity. When the choice of knowing-better yet not-doing is made, that is when the justifications surface. My least favorite and largest waste-of-life example is the saying that "All roads lead to Rome." This means that no matter what you do, you will get the results. This is the theme song of the weak, the cowardly, the quitters and the posers. Unfortunately for them, reality and the standards required to achieve results are inflexible, and until they accept this, they remain stuck.

It is worth noting that, unlike the promise of many religions, you can opt out of your initiation at any time. No higher power will take on the responsibility and beg you to keep going (and no teachers should do this either). Even if the seeker has slammed the door hard, his own inner call can still be heard when the noise quiets down. The tremendous upside for the quitters and posers is that the door can always be reopened, and the path re-committed to when ready. The path is neutral and forgiving in that way. Keep in mind that those who can teach you—and time itself—may not be that forgiving so be careful around your decision to quit.

In the hero's journey examples I used earlier, the protagonist student/seeker shows up at the abode of the mentor/master to undergo education and training. In the favored and popular versions of these stories, the students complete the training and become masters themselves. Most people see themselves in this way. They violently defend their identities as "red pill" people and "initiates," displaying the merit badges and memberships as proof of "leveling up." They insist that they will carry on until the end, and that nothing can or will stop them. Despite their insistence...*why are there so few masters*?

> **Have you ever wondered why so few people cross the gap between student and master?**

My late teacher, Dr. Christopher Hyatt often said that those with the *potential* to "make it" were 1 in 10. (He called them mutants and futants.) Some of his peers thought he was *quite* generous with this estimate and thought it to be more like 1 in 100, if not 1 in 1,000.

Unfortunately, in real life, the fates of seekers are not always the happy endings we see in the movies and stories we aspire to emulate. In our imagination, *we are the ones who "make it" and who go all the way.* Let's continue with the student/temple analogy from Chapter 2 to illuminate the common fates of seekers. Consider that the further down the list, the fewer the people:

1. The average person has no awareness or interest in this type of work and study. This is a great majority of the population.
2. The student never actually shows up to the temple, he simply reads about it and does some sort of "self-initiation," making up the rules and work as he goes—which means that he keeps doing what he was already doing, just with a new vocabulary.
3. The student enters the temple, sees what is really required, and quickly departs, telling himself "this isn't for me." He picks and chooses what suits his comfort zone and personal habits.
4. The student enters the temple, doesn't think or *feel* that the temple and its work align closely enough with his expectations and current level of knowledge and strength. He may feel he is already *better than* those at the temple. He insists that he needn't work *that* hard, and often chooses work that doesn't

offend his ego. Often these students will quit, but not leave. He drags his feet, feels sorry for himself, pouts, and at times lashes out at others.
5. Sometimes the unsuccessful types make it onto the radar—they fill important roles in stories and movies. Often, they become part of the tragic masses, looking on at the success of the student who was once next to him. A few will become "villains," "pirates," "vampires" or some other self-defined term that, in their fantasy, turns their failure into a virtue. They think they get power by being "evil." These people tend to seek to trip up those who persist in their work, and at times will seek "revenge" towards those who "shunned" them in the first place—including parents, teachers, anyone in a position of authority, those more successful and *society in general.*
6. The student enters the temple, begins the work, and sticks it out until he is pressed against his fears, baggage and sacred beliefs. At this point he will often wobble, disengage, and "take a break." Some quit and never return, while other come to their senses and pick it up again. A few realize that the reward and results are worth the short-term suffering and begin to develop some momentum. Some from this smaller group will continue on and "pass the invisible boundary" as Thoreau put it, and become the last, rare type.
7. The final type is the one who continues forward until he finishes the work. (It is worth noting that the work is never really finished, yet there are certain insights that, once attained, cannot be unseen, and certain work, once completed, requires no more effort.) People at this stage move beyond the paradox of the student and the master, gaining enough insight and discernment to invent and/or implement their own techniques and strategies as necessary to deepen and solidify their gains. Momentum is self-sustaining and of a sufficient enough level that he no longer worries about losing his way. When he *knows how to know,* he is no longer dependent upon external validation and often prefers solitude to group work and collective (make-belief) belief systems. Those in this last group will make it as far as they can, and sometimes that is *all the way.*

The Path to Personal Power

> Regardless of the category that you think you fall into,
> the only important question is...
> **What are you willing to ask of yourself?**

Notice that I didn't ask what you want to get out of this for yourself or what you think you need from others.

If you really want to take the red pill and commit to the path of power and self-mastery, then the determining factor is YOU. It is not up to your parents, or the government, or your "group." It is not dependent upon your teacher or guide, and their style and/or limitations. Besides the roadmap, techniques and pointers (which comprises most of this book)—YOU will decide how far you go. It will be YOU and YOU alone who makes the decision to opt out, or to keep going. It is up to you to build up the necessary resources, stomach, strength, commitment, self-acceptance and self-love to reach these lofty aspirations.

> **~ EXERCISE ~**
> What are you willing to ask of yourself?
> Do you understand that if or when you opt out...
> is completely up to you?

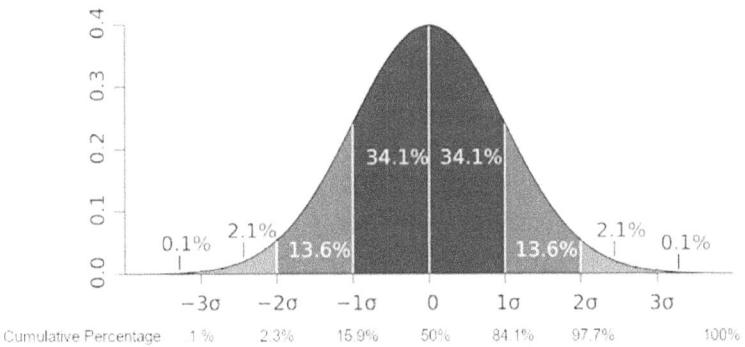

I think that most students of the work fit into the normal distribution or bell curve. Consider the statistics in terms of success in life provided through the work. As you move to the right you are making progress in creating yourself and your life into a work of art, including less suffering and increased success in multiple areas.

By studying the picture, you can see that a good deal of the population is centered around an "average life," and that 50% of the population is below the average. As you move from the left to the right, you can add the cumulative population. By the time you reach one positive standard deviation (σ), you have surpassed 84%. Consider how good life would be if all of the areas in life that are important to you were at that level. Using the student/temple analogy from earlier in the chapter, I would consider group #1 this point as well. That puts 84% of people not having any knowledge and/or interest in the work. I would rank the students that reach #6 and #7, the ones who actually get things done at the second standard deviation around 98%. That means only 2 in 100 reach that level.

It is useful to remember that the more you ask of yourself, the further you move to the right. This can come in handy when you want to quit.

The far-right side (3rd standard deviation) of the bell curve is small and at the far end for a reason…because most people give up when the going gets tough. Only a select few go further. Only those truly committed to mastery go all the way. Those who are outstanding are further to the right than you think. Those who reach mastery as laid out in this book are well into the 3rd standard deviation, which accounts for only one tenth of one percent.

The *how* of the path—the actual real-world work that is necessary—is, at times, unpleasant. It is often a direct affront to your ego. In fact, I have yet to meet someone who wasn't surprised at what it takes, and equally surprised that the work and its effects are different than what they've read. There is much written about "cosmic crackups" and "the dark nights of the soul"—from warnings to survival guides. A lot of this is over-dramatization, yet you need to be ready and learn how to navigate through the unpleasantness and uncertainty you encounter. Having a big enough *why* is what will keep you going and keep you from quitting when the going gets tough.

> "He who has a WHY to live can bear almost any HOW."
> — Friedrich Nietzsche

The Path to Personal Power

If you want to travel the path and go all the way...if you *really* want to take the red pill.... you need to be well acquainted with your *why*. Your *why* will need to be more than mere curiosity, lukewarm desire or that it sounds like a good idea because your buddy is trying to talk you into doing it with him. Your *why* needs to be more than a fair-weather whim. It needs to be large enough and strong enough to sustain your efforts until you arrive. Your *why* needs to go beyond "nice-to-have" and reach to "MUST HAVE." You need to get your *why* in order, keep it charged up, and keep it in front of you, in plain sight, at all times.

Those who wish to overcome their nature and fully awaken must be willing to pay the price in full, in advance, without guarantees... *every time.*

> **This is why so few cross the gap from student to master.**

Chapter 5
Discernment

What is "discernment"? The dictionary has it as "good judgement, knowledge, experience, shrewdness and insight."

In my estimation, discernment is the roommate of wisdom—both the cause and precursor to wisdom, as well as the byproduct of it. Discernment is one of the most important, needed and prized attainments of the path, and simultaneously the decoder ring of the path. It will help you to avoid cutting off your nose to spite your face.

Discernment is knowing *how* to know and knowing when you don't know. It helps you to **know** the difference between what is truly self-enhancing and what is self-diminishing—especially in the long-term perspective of the path.

Discernment increases as you refine your connecting link to your intuition, yet remains unmoved by your desire for things to come easily. It is the force multiplier and turbo boost of the path. It also works as your internal compass for the path when you are wondering which way to go at a fork in the road.

Discernment is the quality that makes the most difference in terms of more accurately traveling the path when the signs are faint and not easy to read. It is the hearing aid for the faintest inner voice.

Example: Consider a dog. Take seven dog bowls and label each for a day of the week, Monday through Sunday. Fill each of these bowls with dog food. What does the dog do? It eats all of them in one sitting.

We think we are smarter and more evolved than the dog. Yet, how many people know the "right thing" to do and then do otherwise? Everyone knows "how" to lose weight. Everyone knows that brushing and flossing their teeth is necessary for oral hygiene. The dog can't help its nature. Can humans?

We all have a self-serving bias. The real question is: Which "self" is it serving?

When you make a purchase, you become more likely to defend the purchase, even in the face of contradictory facts (the "endowment effect"). When people are married for a while and the relationship is no longer working, they often say "I can't get divorced, I've invested so much!" (the "sunk cost fallacy"). Why confront the ego when you can waste a lot more time and money by NOT changing your mind and cutting your losses? Are you aware of your mental biases, such as the examples in this paragraph?

Have you ever been walking down the sidewalk, caught an edge with your foot and tripped violently? What is the first reaction? To look around murderously for someone to blame and punish? To curse the sidewalk and everyone who has ever been involved in its upkeep? Some people live their entire lives like this without ever seeing the pattern or knowing there is a different perspective.

Without discernment, it is very difficult to determine the motivation for a decision. Is it made from a defensive stance (to defend and preserve the ego) or out of true interest? Many people become doctors and lawyers because that's what their parents did or wanted them to do. Did you choose your own religion, political affiliation or favorite place to live because it serves YOU?

Young children are not left to their own devices because they don't know what's good for them and what isn't. How many adults should really be left to their own devices? Look at yourself closely. How often do you "know-better" and still engage in not-doing it?

~ EXERCISE ~
Write down the following:
Your own personal distinction between "playing to win" and "playing to not lose?"
How and when have you acted these out at key moments in your life?

When you have discernment, good things happen. You know when you are pulling the wool over your own eyes. You catch yourself, laugh about it, learn your lesson and move forward. You don't drive down long dead ends on your way to self-mastery and power. You don't become a doctor or lawyer for the wrong reasons. You don't marry the wrong person for the wrong reasons. You change your mind when you get new information.

It is often said that "You don't know what you don't know." Discernment is the solution to this. Discernment is friends with humility, which the ego despises. Discernment helps you not drive off a cliff or get stuck in a loop on the way to your mastery. At some point you will need to make decisions on the path about which way to go. Discernment helps you to *know that you know* and, at worst case, helps you turn around quickly and not waste precious years and resources.

At some point on the path you are going to need to make important decisions on your own. At some point **YOU** become the decoder ring. How will you know?

One of my favorite techniques is to look at someone who has done something masterful or ingeniously figured something out and ask the following questions: "How did he know to look for this or see this? What prompted and preceded this understanding?"

Chapter 6
Learning How to Learn (Again)

Learning is typically *thought of* as what takes place in childhood and/or at school. This is compulsory education, and it is often a legal requirement. Despite the obvious failures in the educational system, there is another shortcoming: the system does not teach how to re-evaluate its basic assumptions, nor how to transcend the system. It also does not instill much personal accountability and responsibility.

In the context of personal power, the learning we are talking about is post-compulsory—it is beyond what is required legally and socially. This means that the status quo and the social goals of getting along and doing what everyone else is doing need to be surpassed. The common standards of success must be surpassed, let alone self-awareness, psychological and spiritual development. It also means that **what** we learn, the areas of content themselves we normally associate with learning, must also be re-evaluated and expanded.

The following four-category model of learning is based on Jacques Delors' four pillars of education for the future, which also implies the idea of lifelong learning.

- Understanding: Going beyond the memorization of data and the collection of facts and ideas. Developing the ability of critical thinking and applying it to concepts, contexts and probabilities.
- DOing: Developing skills and abilities to engage in work of all kinds. Increasing your resilience, stamina and capacity for work. Getting out of your comfort zone.
- Relating: Developing mutually beneficial relationships with others, understanding social and unwritten contracts and balancing individuality with the give-and-take of relationships.

- BEing: Developing self-awareness and personal self-development. Expanding your knowledge and understanding of that which is beyond the herd experience. The ability to be in silence, to understand your existence beyond mental concepts, language and categorization. Meditation and self-inquiry to come to know your true self.

As you look at the categories, you will notice that this model is more encompassing than normal social standards and thus more robust. If you strive to continue the duration of learning until the day you die, then you are giving yourself a competitive advantage in the game of life.

> **~ EXERCISE ~**
> Look at the 4 Pillars of Learning and write down one new thing you can do in each area, and two things for the area you typically have paid the least attention to.

One can argue the merits of specialization vs. generalization in education and learning, both in traditional schooling and across the four categories above. Do you see yourself taking pride in knowing a lot about a lot of things, or in being an expert in one or two areas? Robert Heinlein, the author of *Stranger in a Strange Land,* is known for saying that "Specialization is for insects." The opposite of this is the saying "Jack of all trades, master of none." There have been a few hyper-focused individuals who have made significant contributions to the sciences and technology. The cost of extreme hyper-focus may be poor health and damaged relationships. The paradox becomes more clear if you ask yourself what does education and learning serve to enhance? If your answer is your career in the field of cancer research, specialization makes sense. If your answer is to have a happy and balanced life, then your degree of specialization might be lower. The paradox becomes still more clear if you ask what is the purpose of posing specialization against generalization. It is mostly useful as a weapon in defending your position and inclination. You are better off figuring out what level of specialization works to best ensure you reach your goals.

The Path to Personal Power

How you define success in life is up to you. I would argue that it is not a bad plan to seek **more** of both broader generalization **and** deeper specialization *than the average person*. I would encourage you to look at your own motivation about what that balance is, and *why* it is. If you are a linear thinker and a great engineer, you may avoid interpersonal relationships because of your *comfort zone* but justify the avoidance with some other reason. When I work with people like this in corporate America, 99% of the time their professional and personal lives are significantly enhanced by adding in balance and forcing them to develop awareness and skills in the areas outside their comfort zone. Your having a tendency does not justify ignoring your weak areas. Self Mastery does not accept your fears and discomfort as a reason to limit and/or define yourself.

Learning implies not-yet-knowing. For some people the wobbliness of "not-yet-knowing" and/or "not-good-at-it-yet" triggers shame and anxiety. This is a *learned* response. Recall something you were fascinated with as a child—something you couldn't wait to get your hands on. I recall my love for bicycles and learning how to ride. I couldn't wait to ride. I was nervous, fearful and excited. It gave me a sense of freedom. I fell off plenty of times, rode into the bushes and bumped into the car in the driveway. Thoughts of that bicycle consumed me at the dinner table as I nursed my scrapes and bruises. As soon as dinner was over, I was back on my bicycle until dark.

Compare this with the common experience of adult learning. We can easily become self-conscious about our shortcomings (things we have not yet learned or gotten good at) and avoid the wobbles we once couldn't wait to have! This is why it is important that we embrace learning and re-learn how to learn. Learning is another way to say *changing*. Change is *mandatory* on the way to self-mastery and personal power.

~ EXERCISE ~
Pick a physical skill to learn and work on it for 5 to 10 minutes a day by using a timer.
Make notes on your internal self-talk and emotions around not being good at it when you make mistakes.
Juggling is a perfect example for this exercise.

Chapter 7
Adopting an Effective Learning Stance

Learning and progressing often includes a good amount of un-learning. This is best done by rigorously checking your assumptions, defining your terms and asking questions of those who have done more than you and who are getting the results you want. Specific behaviors, accurate measurement and feedback are also invaluable. If you can adopt the stance of an objective scientist who is passionate about potential discoveries and their implications, you have a good footing. If you have a thin skin and big, undisciplined ego, then learning and un-learning are going to sting a little.

Learning happens through study. **Becoming a good student** is about developing an effective learning stance. The more you can do this, the further and faster you progress. The better you get at the learning process (and get out of your own way), the less time it takes to enrich yourself and your life. If you can't (more accurately *won't)* get out of your own way in your own efforts, then you "get to" slow down the process dramatically or stay stuck where you are. For each of the points below, I can almost guarantee that ten years from now you will look back and completely agree. You may also wish you had engaged in the process even more fully and quickly. Some people take a long time to get into the pool, others get over themselves quickly and jump in. There is no right or wrong, but there is a timer running down on your life, so if you value your life…tick tock, tick tock.

Prepare to drop your precious sense of "self." One of my favorite quotes is from Richard Bandler, who said "Why be yourself when you can become something worthwhile?" This may sound harsh, and it is harsh…if you are sentimental about the past and holding on to your precious, less-than-optimal sense of self and its lackluster results. Becoming something more worthwhile is the whole point. You don't see butterflies weeping over their discarded cocoons—you see them stretching their beautiful wings and getting on with the adventure of life.

You cannot change by not-changing. You cannot reach second base without leaving first. Learning implies change. At some point you need to *DO differently*. At some point, when you get into a familiar situation and feel your same-old feelings you are going to need to *DO differently* despite all that has come before.

Assume you don't know: Learning implies that one DOES NOT YET KNOW. How could you know if you haven't been there/done that? It's impossible, so let it go. Being a know-it-all is a defense mechanism for not being good-enough. I know plenty of unsuccessful and stuck "know-it-alls." They are annoying. Best to avoid them, lest you become one.

It's OK to not know: Since you can't know beforehand, you aren't (and shouldn't be) expected to know beforehand. If someone hassled you in the past for not-knowing, then that's on them, not on you. The best attitude is along the lines of "I have little to no idea, can you show me how?"

Let go of the need to be complete and perfect. You will never be perfect. Perfection is the defense to not being "good enough." *YOU* decide if you are good enough, leave yourself alone, and get on with learning. Being pushed by a mentor/teacher is not the same as getting hassled by your parents and other authority figures. You are where you are, and you are planning on getting somewhere better, regardless of how you got here. You did the best you could with what you had, and now you are looking to do even better as you look and move forward. Period. There's a wise old saying I often use in my corporate work, which is "Don't let perfection screw up excellence!"

Minimize the need to impress others and show and tell what you know. It is necessary to do a little of this to bring your teachers/mentors up to speed on your progress. Often there is a tendency to over-share your prior learning and accomplishments. Sometimes this is done to "save face." Check yourself to see if this is helping the learning process or is just padding your ego.

Learn how to let go and be helped. Don't try to control everything, just let go. Allow yourself to be steered. Allow yourself to be shown how to see new things and do new things. Asking for help and being open to help is the shortcut.

Learn how to listen and take feedback. This is one of my favorite predictors of growth, change and success. Defensiveness around feedback only prolongs the process. Feedback is a gift. Often people view feedback as criticism and a personal attack. Instead, learn to *not* take it personally and simply work on the skill under review. It is difficult to improve without measurement. If you suck at playing the piano, it is not a measurement of your absolute value as a human being.

I have a colleague who taught me how to master receiving feedback. At one point, a client called him an asshole. His response? "Yes, I've heard that before. Thanks for pointing it out, and I appreciate that because it's not easy to say. Would you please share with me specifically how I was being an asshole so I can learn from that?" His client's jaw was on the floor. This started a great conversation and further built their relationship. When I asked him how he was able to hold that perspective when put under pressure he replied, "I am an idiot at times just like all of us, and at some point instead of defending it I just gave up and decided to use criticism and feedback as opportunities to improve. We all continue to make mistakes, but this approach allows me to grow faster and I'm actually able to laugh at myself and enjoy it, which means I'm not getting all anxious and stressed out about it or defending it and making it worse. So, what if I make a mistake?"

> You cannot accurately plan a route to a destination if you aren't honest about where you are **right now**.
>
> Your destination is self-mastery and personal power.
>
> Do you want it? Then learn how to shut up, listen, take feedback and apply it.

Let go of the NEED to "know." Sometimes the learning process works better if it is not explained in advance. Many students demand to know the "purpose" of each maneuver and exercise. It is not up to the students to "know better" and pick and choose between tasks in order to reach a certain goal. Thinking that you know impedes your ability to stay in the moment and concentrate on the task at hand.

The Path to Personal Power

Much of this work is subtle. You don't need to understand **how** hypnosis works to utilize it.

Drop the conditions and the need for a guarantee. Many people get caught up in placing conditions on the work. They want to reach mastery, but only as long as "X" isn't disturbed. You cannot steal second base without leaving first. At some point you have to go into the unknown, because what you are really looking for is not contained in the known. There is a leap of faith involved along the path. Many fears will surface, and you need to be willing to sacrifice your preconceptions and imagined solutions for the sake of real attainment.

Drop your preconceptions and expectations. Everyone has preconceptions, expectations and notions. If you expect the answer to come in a certain way, and it does not align to your imagination when it does come, you will miss it. You might even throw it out. Remember the saying "don't throw pearls before swine" (because they do not realize their value and eat them)? A better way to rephrase this is to encourage you not to be the swine—don't start out knowing better and throw away what you don't yet understand and thus cannot value. People think that the attainments of their work need to match their expectations. Learn to reset your pre-conceived notions and your expectations. If you look into what they were, you will learn much about yourself and your patterned responses to the unknown, to learning (not-knowing), and how you defend your ego by avoiding being wrong or incorrect.

Be bold and brave. Take some risks. Be powerful enough to assume that you are incorrect and that you might be completely turned around. Be willing to state that you have no idea and that you were heading in the wrong direction. When you are trying new things, you will make some mistakes. Mistakes are a natural part of learning. Seek out opportunities to grow and stretch. Ask for what you want and for more than you *think* you deserve.

Don't take yourself and the work so seriously. Have fun. Be joyful. Lighten up. It's much easier to do deep and meaningful work if you keep it light. I often remind people that we are all monkeys jumping up and down, carrying on about where the banana went. The purpose of the work is to be self-enhancing, and while it is not always easy or pleasant, difficulties and over-seriousness are also not guarantees of effectiveness and importance.

Drill all the way through. Do thorough work, and work until you are finished. You might need to read a book three times to understand it. You might need more practice and repetitions than you think. The current meme of 10,000 hours of repetition until you reach mastery may hold true for you. It may take less, and it may take twice as long at times. Keep at it. Persistence is more of a predictor of success than inherent gifts.

Don't pay too much attention to the differences of others. Everyone has different strengths, weaknesses, proclivities, gifts and blind spots. Everyone has to do their own work, putting in more time and effort in some areas than others. Worrying about what is "fair" and what comes easier to others is a waste of time. It doesn't change the amount of work that *you* have to put in to reach your goals. Best to get on with it and to focus on what you need to make it happen. Comparing yourself to others is less helpful to your progress than it is to your bruised ego.

Develop and cultivate a sense of curiosity, wonder and possibility. Adults often seem to lose the desire to learn and do something new. More often they want to avoid looking bad. Learning requires being comfortable with a certain amount of inaccuracy and wobble. Some examples are skateboarding, riding a bike, learning an instrument and juggling. Adults tend to prefer and enjoy the resolution and stability of all things that were at one time awkward and embarrassing. If this becomes too much of a habit, learning decreases and stagnation sets in. Are you willing to dance like no one's watching in order to pursue your version of mastery?

Pay attention to what you avoid. Take note of how and where you lower your standards, make excuses, hesitate and avoid anxiety and discomfort. The areas where this happens are important to a part of you, and playing tug-of-war with it does not work. Use these development areas to your advantage. They can tell you a lot about yourself and any conflicting values and double binds that you have in between your ears.

Seek to increase your learning agility. The more you are learning, the better you get at learning…meaning faster and more enjoyable. The more you learn through *doing* and practice, the more skill and knowledge you develop. *The more you engage in the learning process, the more you increase your capacity to do the work.*

Seek to avoid the self-serving bias of the ego. If learning was easy and pleasant then we would approach it faster and more wholeheartedly and avoid it less. Think about how your preferences and excuses serve to protect your ego. This is one root of self-sabotage. This mechanism protects your ego at the expense of your potential. The more you learn to get over yourself, the easier life becomes.

Take notes and keep a journal. The act of writing has power in it as it helps you learn and helps you to pick up where you last left off. It takes a lot of work to acquire self-knowledge and awareness. Why be careless and take the chance of forgetting what you have worked hard to learn and discover? As you come across new ideas, write them down. You may have to cover material several times before it sinks in. If you have your work, ideas and discoveries written down you can't lose them. Consider answering the questions that are posed in this book—they aren't rhetorical.

Special Note: Realize how much you are siding with the author and pointing out all those "other people" for whom these messages are intended. You must develop the strength and awareness to realize that **YOU** are the one who needs to absorb these concepts as they relate to you…all of them. The entire book is about **YOU**.

~ EXERCISE ~
Re-read the Special Note above, and pay attention to how many times you have and/or will think of yourself as "better than others."

Chapter 8
Teachers

There are times when you will need the assistance of others to make progress. Without the guidance of those who have gone before you, your progress will be random and spotty. Working on your own, you may spend years traveling in the wrong direction or heading down a dead-end path. Working with the wrong person may also cost you several years traveling in the wrong direction and validating the *teacher's* dead-end path. Successfully navigating the Teacher/Student relationship is a necessity.

Having discipline on the path is important. What comes to mind when you think of the word *discipline*?

The common definition of discipline is the practice of training people to obey rules or a code of conduct, using punishment to correct disobedience. This definition leaves out some important information and doesn't seem very fun or inviting. Let's also look at the common definition of *disciple*: "A follower or student of a teacher, leader or philosopher."

There are some problems with these definitions. Who sets the code of conduct, and what is its purpose or end goal? At what point does the student himself set the goals and the necessary code of conduct? A one-down position is implied for the student, especially when you have an "obey or be punished" perspective.

Instead of those common definitions, I want you to consider an important perspective that will help your travel immensely:

> You are a disciple of the PATH, not solely of a teacher.

You are primarily a disciple of the *path*…a path of all things self-enhancing. A teacher can focus your attention on blind spots and point you in useful directions, but he cannot magically pass learning and bestow benefits to you.

Here are a few thoughts around teachers that may prove beneficial to both students and teachers. You are responsible for showing up, for being a good student and for your results. This means that you are responsible for your persistence and practice and fully understand that "if it's going to be, it's up to me."

Teachers should consider themselves as ahead of you on the path, not better than you. One-up, one-down is seldom a useful stance. Teachers may have great skills, awareness and results, but that does not make them "better"—although it should earn them respect and the benefit of the doubt.

Expect a value-for-value exchange for their knowledge, experience and tailored help. It is not unrealistic to expect to pay for services. Some teachers value commitment, eagerness and user-friendliness more than others, and that in-and-of-itself is an exchange for value. The investment you make in a teacher is an investment in *yourself,* not an investment in them. This is an easily missed point: if a student is not willing to invest in himself and demands something for free, then there is a deeper issue. People do not value that which is given away for free.

Teachers are not required to teach, and have no social, ethical or moral obligation to help others for free, or to help them at all for that matter. Be careful with what you think you are entitled to.

Teachers should not just sell the process, but also possess the *promise* that the process is set up to achieve. They should possess the attributes and abilities you are striving for yourself. For the most part good teachers don't ask students to do things they haven't done or are unwilling to do themselves.

A good teacher is willing to tell you the truth even if it means temporarily breaking rapport and offending your ego. They will not hide your lessons from you or tell you what you would like to hear. Learning how to accept discomfort, pick yourself up and heal are all parts of the journey. Premature rescuing and pampering do little more than strengthen your dependency on others.

Don't expect your teachers to be perfect and fully evolved. Being ahead of you on the path is enough for you to be able to learn from them. Focusing on their flaws and shortcomings is, for the most part, a projection of your own fears and/or an ego-defense mechanism.

Discernment is also critical in selecting who to work with, how long to work with them, and in what manner to work with them. I can't stress enough that you don't know what you don't know, and your childlike ego will want to choose what is comfortable. Many people hang around the "rainbows and unicorns" gurus who like to talk about white light and positivity. Those gurus believe in their own bullshit, as do their students. Do an internet search for videos about "no touch" martial arts pitted against reality to see what happens. The fields of personal development and spirituality are no different when it comes to developing magical powers, personal power and enlightenment. The interesting question is: Why do these frauds have so many students? It is because people would rather *feel good* than know the truth. The further you go on this path the more this is true, because the truths of life are not what we were told as children.

Discernment is also important because there may come a time when a student needs a different perspective or outgrows a teacher. Just keep in mind the tricks your mind and ego will play on you in order to stay in your comfort zone and have your preconceptions and beliefs validated. A good teacher will understand and will be willing to have a dialogue about these conundrums as they will value your growth over being followed.

Towards the end of the path, you will need to have enough discernment, technique and self-accountability to make it the rest of the way. Your real teacher/master is *the part of you where the inner calling comes from*. This inner guide is not a useful focus at the beginning of the path. It is good to listen for it, to honor and acknowledge it when it shows up, and seek to strengthen your relationship to it. It is a very faint voice at first, and the problem with this is that most people tend to focus on the voice of their ego, while telling themselves it's their inner guide, and using that as a justification to do all kinds of nonsense. These people are the "deluded holy ones," fundamentally no different from the average population aside from telling themselves a different tale with a mystical new vocabulary.

As questions and concerns come up around your relationship to those who can help, you should respectfully bring them up for discussion. How these questions are answered or avoided will help you make choices around who is a good fit.

Understanding

Chapter 9
Why Believe in Believing?

Why believe in believing? When you *know* something, belief is not necessary. Believing is accepting something as true without proof. On the other hand, knowledge consists of facts and information gained through experience. For example, if I want to know the square footage of my living room, I measure the length and width then multiply those numbers together. This comes up with a factual answer every time. Believing is not necessary in this case.

Unless you look into the *process* of belief you will move through life like a pre-programmed robot, which is the opposite of what we are trying to do here. What exists in the conceptual world does not necessarily exist in reality. Problems that exist in thought do not necessarily exist in reality, but if you are unaware of this, then your inner world will hold you back in the external world.

What are knowledge and beliefs made of? They are made of mental images and internal dialogue with some emotions that quickly follow, serving as "proof." You can observe this yourself in your imagination. Use the idea of measuring the square footage of the room you are in, and then again, the idea of Bigfoot. You can "imagine" both of these. They are made up of thoughts. The issue is that thoughts do not necessarily reflect reality in terms of recordable data and repeatability. Bigfoot cannot be verified, while square footage and the process of solving for square footage can be verified. (It is possible to take the concepts of knowledge and truth down a deep philosophical rabbit hole and get stuck in questions and argument around whether it is truly possible to know anything at all. This is for academics who want to ponder life, not students of power who want to accomplish tangible things in their lives.)

People believe in Bigfoot and UFOs. They make mental images about them and internal dialogue to go with them. They may have very strong feelings about their beliefs. They may argue and fight and kill over them...which means they do so over the differences in the *content of thought* **and** *the strength of their emotions*...without ever thinking that the *process* of believing in-and-of-itself is pointless and yields nothing. This is an abuse of the power of imagination.

If you agree with me, then you will not mind giving up all of your beliefs and dare to live without them. What would change? What cannot be proven may or may not exist. I am suggesting that your energy will be better served by working on yourself and in the areas of your life where belief is not needed. The other choice is to live as an idiot serving your beliefs instead of your personal reality. Yes, the word "serving" is harsh. You cannot hold beliefs without them using up some of your energy.

At one time some people believed the world was flat and were afraid to sail off the edge of the world. They could have decided to ***stop believing in belief itself*** and just gotten busy with their work—sailing. They could have decided they would deal with the edge of the world *if* they found it. This would have freed up energy that could have been used to make faster progress and yield more results on the open sea.

Experiment: Sit down, put both feet firmly on the floor. Feel the floor underneath your feet. Look at your feet on the floor.

Do you KNOW that your feet are on the floor? THINK about and consider the following carefully:

> ***There is no "believing" necessary for you to KNOW that your feet are on the floor.***

There is no faith needed to know this.
There are no schools or schools of thought needed.
Politics is not needed.
Religion is not needed.
Experts, scientists, doctors and lawyers are not needed.
Words are not needed.
Inner dialogue is not needed.
The past is not needed.
A guarantee is not needed.
Concepts are not needed.
Permission is not needed.

> Direct experience is enough—it is all that is needed.

Few people ever look into the non-reality of their beliefs. If you do not know what causes you to suffer, how can you be rid of it? If you do not know what controls you, how can you be free of it?

> **~ EXERCISE ~**
>
> Think about the beliefs you hold about yourself.
>
> What are your personal limits?
> Are you worthwhile?
> Are you deserving of love?
> Are you a no-good-shit?
>
> Is it possible you have mistaken your beliefs as absolute truths? Are you open to the facts that these concepts do not exist?
>
> If they do not exist, might you get free of the weight and despair these concepts bring you?

Chapter 10
Transparency

You do not need to swallow the philosophy discussed in this book blindly. It is based on understanding and pragmatics and thus can be transparent to the student This means there is nothing to hide, and you can learn *through your own experience* that the path leads to greater power, understanding and less suffering. Because you can trust it without worrying about others' agendas, you can instead focus your efforts on trusting yourself and on the work at hand.

The Path has nothing to hide. There are no secrets. There are no extra levels. You are the wizard behind the curtain. Because of its transparency the path hides in plain sight.

There is great power and momentum available through this level of transparency. At first glance you might think that it leaves the system more vulnerable to criticism or plagiarism, but that is not the case. In fact, the opposite is true: its vulnerability *is* its strength. This is important, because *your* vulnerability is also *your* strength.

Your ability to be ok with who you are and where you find yourself **right now,** without editing yourself, is your power. This is the first step towards real progress. Regardless of what you admit to yourself, the path sees you as you are. There is no shame in not-yet-knowing or not-there-yet. You are a work in progress. How other people think of you and of your path—especially if they are on a different path—is irrelevant.

Chapter 11
The Black Box

It is interesting to compare the problems people have and their high levels of suffering, with the amount of understanding they have about what is really going on inside their heads and their nervous systems. Most people know much more about fashion trends, tv shows, sports stats and politics than about their own psychological functioning...let alone real techniques to change functioning for the better.

Even for those who take an interest in self-development and healing, very little is known about how things really work. Certainly there is a great deal of research which can move us in the right direction, but very little of it has been distilled into methods for change.

For most people, how their nervous system takes in data and translates it into emotional states and behaviors is completely unknown to them. This makes their own nervous system a black box which operates outside their awareness and as such is never questioned.

A black box is the decision-making part of a system. Data goes in and results are spit out without any knowledge of its inner workings (the mechanism itself that makes the decision is unknown and out of sight as if it were inside a black box.)

Often a stock trading system is considered a black box system. Market conditions are monitored and buy and sell signals come out. As these are proprietary and give a competitive advantage to the *inventor/creator/salesperson,* the algorithm is deliberately hidden.

If you don't know about radiators and anti-freeze when your car overheats, then you don't know how to fix the problem. The engine cools down and works for a while only to have the same problem recur. Most people do not tolerate this from their cars, yet they tolerate it of their own nervous system and suffer needlessly their entire lives. Without some working knowledge of your self, you can only travel so far down the path to mastery before overheating.

The Path to Personal Power

When the psychological functioning of our selves is a black box, it is very difficult to pursue self-development. How can you change a limiting belief or stop feeling bad about yourself if you don't know how it's happening? What's worse is that the people selling you self-esteem, hopes and ego-boosts don't care if you don't know, because you can't test the efficacy of what they are selling. The real kicker is that what you end up doing often makes your problems worse. This is why it is so important to take the time to understand yourself—so you can make real progress.

The best way to understand the black box is to open it up as much as possible and take a look into it. Be forewarned, many of the components inside do not correspond to what you have been taught to believe. Many of the inputs and outputs, the beliefs, emotions and behaviors serve other people who may not be interested or supportive around your "waking up." The "occult" was hidden for hundreds of years for a reason. Galileo was put under house arrest for the remainder of this life for not supporting the idea (or the people backing it) that the sun revolved around the earth.

Chapter 12
So, Tell Me About Your Childhood

The title of this chapter might evoke what you would expect to hear from a bearded therapist with a German accent when you visit his office for the first time. I propose that a better way to start off is "Let **me** tell **you** about *your* childhood." Most people mistakenly think that the experiences of their childhood are to blame for their being stuck in life. What is far more important is the impact of our developmental process *regardless of the experiences.* The prolonged experience of childhood presents difficulties for every human being on this planet. You do not have to have had a "bad" childhood or horrible parents to be stuck with the limitations of our species.

What limitations, you ask? There are several quirks which we will be exploring, along with our mistaken conclusions and judgments about ourselves, our value (or lack of it) and the "way things work." By taking apart the black box, you can begin to operate under a different set of rules—ones that are in your favor.

Without understanding how neurological mechanisms work, it is very difficult to know what data to pay attention to, what is "real," what data to use in making decisions and most importantly, how to change the mechanism itself. A curious example: a "full grown and mature" adult has a dream about catching his spouse cheating and then, upon waking, becomes angry with him for the rest of the day (true client story). This is not indicative of logical functioning, nor is it useful for their relationship.

> **That which is not seen and not known cannot be understood or handled and therefore continues to haunt you.**

The Path to Personal Power 61

From birth we are exposed to a world we struggle to understand and function in. We do the best we can with what we have: limited information, poor instruction, overwhelming emotions and a partially developed brain. We do the best we can in the contexts we find ourselves in, which include "grown-ups" with their own fears, beliefs, agendas and superstitions. We use our undeveloped minds to categorize ourselves, others and our experiences. We use those little, partially developed minds to draw conclusions about ourselves, other people, our world and the rules that govern us. We do all of this at our own peril, unbeknownst to ourselves.

As discussed in the previous chapter, the development and functioning of the human nervous system is almost completely unknown to most people. Data is taken in through the senses, processed, and out pops emotions and behavior. Obviously, this is an over-simplification, but it is enough to start with.

Issue: The adult brain, or front brain, which is the thinking and logical part of the brain, does not begin to develop until age 5. It cannot *begin* to perform critical thinking and logical functions until age 7–7½, and takes until age 20 to fully mature (if worked properly).

Impact: Age 0–7: The brain has not developed enough and therefore **cannot** perform logical functions, including: 1) The ability to shift attention and frame of reference; understanding multiple possible frames of reference, contexts and probabilities; 2) The ability to understand measurements and values; 3) The ability to understand cause-and-effect, plausibility and reversibility; 4) Reality testing.

Result: Without logical abilities, the child makes decisions, judgements, conclusions, assigns causality and meaning, and justifies all of this primarily though instincts and emotions which come from what used to be considered "lower" parts of the brain.

Children live in a more or less binary world: stop/go, yes/no, advance/retreat, good/bad, all/nothing, win/lose. Without the ability to evaluate these concepts on a continuum or in a matrix of contexts and probabilities (an ability which few adults possess either), the world can be a scary place to navigate. The concept of "maybe" is mostly unavailable in early stages of development, as it involves evaluating a matrix of different variables and presuppositions.

The question "Are you a good boy?" in early stages of development is a yes/no and all-or-nothing proposition. The nervous system utilizes pain and pleasure to steer behavior in a red-light/green-light fashion well before logical capacity develops. Devoid of any critical thinking or evaluation, "Good" is associated early on with pleasure, relaxation and satisfaction, just as "Bad" is associated with anxiety, pain and fear. Pain and pleasure are easily labeled as good and bad and are for the most part indistinguishable from the labels *because the child cannot sufficiently (if at all) distinguish self from emotion.*

There is little functional difference in the child's understanding of good/bad and pain/pleasure. Coupled with their inability to distinguish self from emotions and feelings, *the programming is set early on for full allegiance to the concepts of good and bad and both the real and perceived rewards and punishments of each.* The net result is that a child's behavior is easily steered by good/bad and pain/pleasure. Children fear "badness." The pain due to the resulting loss of status, acceptance, love and ultimately the loss of absolute (metaphysical) value are too great to be withstood or ignored. This same learning process also makes programming preferred beliefs, fears, rules and just about any nonsense relatively easy by simply *making them feel* good or bad. This is a cheap way to enforce behaviors and beliefs because it is easier than having the intelligence and resources to properly raise a child. It also has long lasting effects which can be difficult to change, keeping me steadily employed with corporate and private clients.

Emotions easily overwhelm children, and because the emotions are so powerful and they cannot yet reason, *emotions serve as proof.* Therefore, the feeling of "bad" is analogous to *being* "bad." Emotions also serve as justification for behavior and for reality testing. "I don't feel like it" or "I just felt like it" is enough to justify behavior or the lack of it. The monsters under the bed *feel* real enough.

To understand why this discussion is so important, let's connect the information in the previous paragraphs with the original impact statement and expand the scope of the result.

The Path to Personal Power

Impact: Age 0–7: The brain has not developed enough and therefore **cannot** perform logical functions, including: 1) The ability to shift attention and frame of reference; understanding multiple possible frames of reference, contexts and probabilities. 2) The ability to understand measurements and values. 3) The ability to understand cause-and-effect, plausibility and reversibility. 4) Reality testing.

Result: Without logical abilities, the child makes decisions, judgements, conclusions, assigns causality and meaning, and justifies all of this primarily though instincts and emotions which come from what used to be considered "lower" parts of the brain.

- I am bad because I feel bad. I feel it, therefore it is real and true.
- My parents say I'm bad and I am not capable of questioning the validity of what they say. I cannot comprehend that my parents may be bad themselves and thus cannot take into consideration *the source*.
- I have no way to determine if it's even possible to *BE bad*. I cannot distinguish concepts from reality (plausibility).
- I cannot distinguish whether the concept of bad is an innate *quality* or the result of my behavior. Example: because I have undeveloped coordination, strength and balance I did a bad job of washing the car, and therefore I am bad.

Now, when we add in *reversibility* this starts to get serious. Reversibility is a logical function that allows us to make a change to something, and then change it back to its starting state and restore it. A common example: you make a child a sandwich and it's all good...but...then you put lettuce on it. The child gets upset with this addition and refuses to eat the sandwich. You take off the lettuce and what happens? The sandwich is *still* no good—it has been tainted. It cannot go back to the normal sandwich because the child's mind has not yet developed enough to perform the function of reversibility.

Here's the punchline: *What if you believe you are "bad" and it's not reversible?* You are worried about being bad *forever*. You are worried about being un-love-able. This is shame—the unworthiness of love and fair treatment. This is extremely painful and extremely real for children. The idea of metaphysical value is very important because it controls and shapes us at an early age—and beyond.

> The "possibility" of actually *BEing* bad is called Metaphysical Value. It is a philosophical problem that manifests in a very real way.

The concept of being good or bad is a matter of axiological ethics. We can look at a child (or ourselves) being bad *intrinsically* or *instrumentally*. To be intrinsically good or bad indicates an inherent nature which is out of your control, much like luck or being cursed. To be instrumentally good or bad considers context and the preferences of others. Good or bad *for whom* and *in what context* based on *what set of rules?* Who determines those rules? Is it the individual or a higher authority?

If I said that a child crying on an airplane is bad, then this is an instrumental judgment based on my preference to have silence during my flight. The difference between me and the child is that I can (as an adult who is smart and aware enough) make the distinction between the instrumental *badness* and the idea of intrinsic badness. The child is not inherently bad or made up of the quality of badness because it cries, despite being an inconvenience on an airplane. If I violently spank and scold the child for being bad, I will guarantee that it will interpret this as its own intrinsic badness and its overwhelming emotions will cement this as proof. The child will not assume I am overreacting or being unreasonable and cruel.

It is useful to recognize that from the child's perspective, I am assigning it *bad intrinsic value,* partly because of my authority and partly because the child is not functionally aware of the difference. Children are surrounded by stories of history and religion and constantly live in a dialogue of good or bad that *does not make the distinction* between intrinsic and instrumental value. With *feelings-as-proof* we are sentenced. Without the distinction, we are unaware of the choice. The idea that one might actually be intrinsically bad, without hope of salvation, is very real. We call this idea metaphysical value. The *metaphysical* component comes from the idea that a higher authority *outside of yourself* is denoting and assigning this value, perhaps god or existence itself. Metaphysical, by definition, points to the non-reality of this authority.

Not only do children not make the distinction between intrinsic and instrumental personal value, but neither do adults for the most part. This distinction never crosses their mind. Yet the distinction is very important because it forms the foundation of *why* you should work to stop being limited by guilt, shame and the steering mechanisms of your nervous system. By making the distinction between intrinsic and instrumental personal value, you can stop believing in the concept of "bad intrinsic value." If you know that you are not inherently bad, then you can allow yourself new behavioral options that previously weren't open to you because of the irrational yet real fear of "being bad."

~ EXERCISE ~
What changes would you make in your life,
What opportunities would you pursue,
If you were no longer worried about "being no-good?"

If you can remember times early in your life when you got into big trouble and your parents were angry and disappointed with you, you might remember the terror and panic that you felt. You might remember worrying if things could ever be ok again. The possibility of really being incurably bad, and thus worthless to others, is quite frightening and painful for a child. The result of this condition could be excommunication from the family/tribe.

To protect your life your nervous system pays special attention and remembers emotional extremes. Through thousands of years of evolution, your nervous system has equated higher chances of survival with remaining in the tribe. The chances of dehydration, starvation, freezing to death or being eaten animals are too great on your own.

Playing for life or death and/or permanently valuable/worthless stakes with a not-yet-developed brain and sensitive nervous system is an extremely powerful and random steering mechanism for everyone who goes through the process of human development.

The binary world view of the child also accounts for the attributes and desires he will own and be responsible for. Imagination and the pretend play that arises is considered a sign of healthy development. Children pretend to be doctors and nurses, teachers and soldiers, ballerinas and superheroes. They envision themselves respected and admired by others with status and power. They are also quick to disown and split off the "bad parts" of themselves. They disacknowledge those characteristics so as not to get caught with them, be labeled with them and thus feel guilty (bad) because of them.

Children are quick to bury their own wants and desires when these come into conflict with the need to avoid being "bad" and desire to be "good." This may not be apparent on the surface, because children constantly ask for what they want and test their parents' boundaries. As children are faced with the pain of disapproval from their parents, they give up their wants and desires because they see these as what is causing their "badness."

When viewing the world through this lens, it is easy to see how a belief along the following lines can easily be formed: "I am bad when I get what I want," "I am bad if I don't do what others want," or any of the infinite variations of this.

Children are also quick to align themselves with what their parents *believe*. Often the difference between "Good" and "Bad" comes down to a few simple binary *opinions* of the parents. These include:

1) **Basic sacrifices of parenting.** Are the children disturbing or annoying us, and can/will we handle it appropriately? Any normal developmental task or mistake can be "bad" if it annoys the parents. Examples: Peeing in your pants, refusing to share, not wanting to brush teeth/eat vegetables/go to bed.

2) **Similarity.** Do they dress/look/think/behave like us? Do they believe what we believe? This is an unintelligent and disappointingly pervasive way to make invalid value judgments. Examples: You don't see many parents encouraging the exploration of different religious or political views. It is also not uncommon for parents to discourage their children from exceeding their own standards and accomplishments in terms of education, career, social status, finances and quality relation-

ships. The odds of being the healthy child of obese parents or the clean and organized child of hoarders are slim.

3) The parents' own needs and whims. Often decisions that affect the development of a child are based on a parent's own psychological needs and disposition instead of what is best for their child. Examples: A parent with a personality disorder is unable or unwilling to provide the attention and love needed for the child to develop positive self-regard. Children are discouraged from learning to become self-sufficient because a parent feels "unimportant"—as if this was the child's responsibility. A parent who suffers from addiction is another example of imposing a lifestyle designed to serve adult difficulties onto a child.

The list of unproven, ridiculous or otherwise useless ideas is endless, but may include things such as long-term breast feeding, venomous snake-handling religions, extreme politics and prejudice, poor hygiene, superstition, myth and folk wisdom. (Who declared that the dark ages were over?)

As the adult brain begins to develop and the gains made in cognition get stronger, the child feels that he is "growing up." This *appears* to himself and others to be the case when you look at the abilities and skills that develop. The fact is that although we have access to the skills of the adult brain, the entire mechanism that steered us for our younger years **does not go away or cease to function.** Few people realize or acknowledge how much the lower level functions continue to control them despite their higher-level wishes.

Some of your concepts and beliefs have been redefined as you have grown up. Santa Claus is a great example. At age 8 or 9 someone clues you in that Santa is not actually *real.* You start to think about it, you realize you don't even have a fireplace and that visiting millions of children around the planet between 10 pm and midnight just isn't *plausible.* You feel a little melancholy, and you realize that this is a part of growing up.

How many of your old ideas and beliefs have you deliberately gone back to reevaluate and put into a proper perspective? I would bet that until I proposed this question and presented the idea of the black box and connected some neurological and psychological developmental dots...that you probably haven't gone back at all, at least not deliberately enough. Have you ever really considered that it may not actually be possible to *BE* bad? Have you ever considered that the concept of *being* at all is tenuous at best?

Besides understanding old ideas logically and philosophically, have you sought to behave differently in the world based on your new conclusions? For example, being an anxious clean freak may have been your escape from a dysfunctional childhood, but is it really so important that you hurt those around you whom you love because they missed a spot? Have you considered your relationship towards money? Perhaps you were taught that money was bad because that was your parents excuse for being impulsive and poor.

How many people actually go back and consider all of the split-off parts of themselves—those characteristics that they disowned in order to "fit in"? How many go back and re-integrate these into their lives and regain their natural personality? What about all the beliefs, preferences and decisions based on concepts?

It is highly probable that you have never thought of any of this before. My goal for you is to start to understand the magnitude and pervasiveness of your early and haphazard programming and how human developmental quirks keep you from reaching your potential.

> Very little of this may be *your fault.*
> **All of it is your responsibility.**

Maybe *it is time to consider* a complete and thorough overhaul of your programming.

Chapter 13
Opening Your Eyes

On October 30, 1938, an episode of the *Mercury Theatre on the Air* was broadcast on CBS radio. Narrated by Orson Welles, the adaptation of H.G. Wells' novel *The War of the Worlds* created quite a stir. It is reported that many people, who hadn't heard the "this isn't real" disclaimer fled their homes to avoid the alien invasion. The public was outraged that they had been duped the day before Halloween. (It has been said that the newspapers exaggerated the hysteria to get back at radio for taking away some of their advertising dollars.)

Eleven years later this stunt was repeated in Ecuador, although this time broadcast in Spanish. Panic ensued in the city as police and fire departments rushed to the countryside to engage the invading aliens. When the public found out it was a farce, they turned their attention on the radio station and newspaper who were in on the prank. The riot that ensued resulted in the deaths of six people. The building of a local newspaper that had reported sighting UFOs a few days earlier was burned to the ground.

In both of those stories, people reacted to fiction as if it were real. It's not that they were dumb people from a long time ago, it's because we respond to our internal representations of things *as if* they are real. The story that was told impacted the imaginations of the listeners, and they responded to this imaginary tale in a very real way.

In the moment, in **real time**, we use our sensory organs to take in our surrounding environment. Our eyes, ears, nose, tongue and sense of touch gather data. We can also turn our attention inward to our imagination, where we make internal pictures, movies and dialogue about the data.

Anything that is outside the moment—what just happened, what happened long ago or what we think will happen in the future—is done through memory and imagination, or what is called our internal representational system.

Thinking is never in real time, regardless of how it "seems" or "feels." Ruminating, imagining, remembering, planning, discussing... these all take place inside your head, while the world continues on around you. At best, these internal cognitive activities are an *overlay* on top of in-the-moment reality.

> **The difference between what is in-the-moment and what is representational is an important KEY to understanding and unlocking your potential to evolve.**

In 1933, a few years prior to the radio airing of *War of the Worlds*, philosopher Alfred Korzybski published his book *Science and Sanity*. He discussed how we mirror the external world internally (abstraction), and that "meaning" (semantics) is not inherent in the objects or world-at-large, but within our heads. He is credited for the ideas that "the word is not the thing" and "the map is not the territory." A map is a limited representation of the territory it represents and does not contain all the information about the territory.

René Magritte's painting from 1928–29, *The Treachery of Images*, powerfully drives home that *the representation is not the thing:*

At first glance some may argue that this is indeed a pipe. The text translates to "this is not a pipe." It is more accurate to say that it is a *painting of a pipe,* and more accurate still to say that what you are now looking at is a representation or reproduction of a painting of a pipe. If you close your eyes and see it in your head...this is the representation and abstraction we are talking about and most interested in. It is

The Path to Personal Power

rare to hear someone refer to their inner representation as not real. Rare that anyone thinks about all this at all.

> **The not-thinking about the implications of your internal representations and taking them as "real" IS your problem.**

Why is this a problem? Because internal representations contain too much false data and produce too much of an emotional response. It *steers* us, whether it is "true" or "real" or not.

The internal "map" contains images and internal dialogue *about* the real territory, and it also contains labels, judgements and conclusions and, further, images and dialogue about the labels, judgements and conclusions.

When we see a small spider, our neurology not only interacts with the insect in real time, but also with all the internally stored information, past experiences and hopes/beliefs we have around spiders. The particular spider we are dealing with could very well be a legend amongst all spiders. It could be a rare variation with the longest legs ever previously found in that species. It could be the first spider to communicate in a certain way, or the spider that has traveled the farthest. You wouldn't know because you never thought to look for these things, as it's "just a spider" and thus its unique characteristics are overlooked.

A research scientist might approach the spider with curiosity and amazement, while someone with a spider phobia would have a much different response. What is the difference? It's the same spider! But the internal representation of a spider in a phobic's mind is much different than the one in a scientist's mind. Phobics tend to have very large internal images, with lots of detail. They also tend to be fully involved, rather than dissociated. A spider that is 1/8-inch-long may very well be 10 stories tall in their mind's eye. In their inner map, it may also be making threatening gestures or may be an internal movie that ends up in death. Keep in mind that this internal process happens in a split-second outside of our consciousness.

Which one provokes a bigger emotional response?

This?

Or...

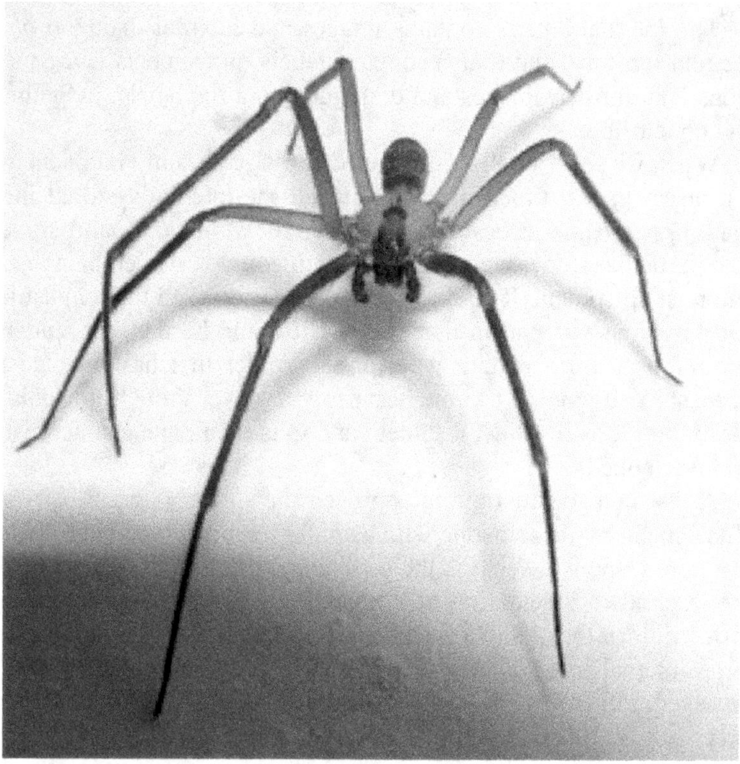

The French philosopher Jean Baudrillard, who wrote *Simulacra and Simulation,* posits that we have become so reliant on the models and the map that we have detached from the reality of which they were created in the first place. Through our media-culture reinforcement, people have become so used to the copies that they live in the map,

The Path to Personal Power 73

rather than in reality. Do you think that the way our neurology works to inflate the internal representations and produce more adrenaline, dopamine, etc. might be the mechanism behind this? The internal representation becomes more real than reality. This is how arachnophobia works. This is how *all* beliefs work.

The science fiction movie *The Matrix* uses this analogy quite well. People are plugged into a mental simulation while their bodies, which have never moved, are used to generate electricity. Few of these people are ever awakened.

The Matrix also illustrates another important point. It's not just that your map may contain distorted and inaccurate information, but it may *not contain enough* information. How do you realize what you don't know? A relevant example is our discussion about our neurological black box. Data is taken in through the senses, it is manipulated and distorted through the internal representational system, which produces feelings that—hold onto your hat folks—make it real and true? Your representational system produces feelings that are proof and also justify your actions?? Oops. Real and true *enough* to kill 6 people in Ecuador. Real and true enough to hate and kill people of other races and ethnicities. Real and true enough to drain the blood of sick people to let out the bad humors (evil spirits) and heal them.

One of the high costs of ignorance about this part of our human nature is intense suffering. Spider phobics tend to suffer greatly when presented with spiders. It takes effort and energy to release enough adrenaline for an adult to jump upon a table and elevate their heart rate and blood pressure to near maximum levels. Fear and depression do not lead to creativity, taking calculated risks and putting yourself out in front of opportunities.

Another high cost of not-knowing the influence of our internal representational system is poor decision making. Making emotional and reactive decisions leads to poor outcomes compared to calculated *responses* to what comes at us. Do you think far enough into the future when making decisions? Decisions to eat poorly, not exercise and act out of impulsive whim often stem from not thinking far enough into the future on how those decisions can negatively affect you.

People throughout history have been willing to kill and be killed based on *belief* in stories and concepts. Think back to *War of the*

Worlds. Think about September 11, Nazi Germany, and most of human history. People kill spiders because they are yucky, and they often readily hate and kill other people as well. The same thing is going on in politics *right now!* Data and solutions are completely overlooked and take a distant back seat to belonging to one tribe while despising the other. Solving problems in *reality* is ignored, while concepts and labels are worshipped.

The most common response I get from the people I present this information to is "I never really thought about it." Never really thought about it, but yet it's going on anyway in the background of your mind, potentially ruining your life. This material is not just for philosophers, it is for every person who is serious about improving themselves and their condition. This mechanism is steering **YOUR LIFE**. Everything we know, believe, value, and hold dear is based on this process, not necessarily on reality. We hold our map, beliefs, conclusions as more important—we worship them and give them fidelity and loyalty—over our potential and our true selves.

People probably never thought to question whether that radio broadcast was real, but they rioted and killed a few people anyway. People don't typically question whether or not what is going on in their heads is real or relevant either. Maybe you should start thinking about it.

Wake the fuck up!

Chapter 14
Imaginary Problems & Limitations

We, as humans, have an incredible ability to use our minds to imagine, invent, create, categorize and strategize. We look to streamline and make things more efficient. We constantly attempt to get more for less.

Unfortunately, our creative ability is quite often misused to create imaginary problems based on the concepts we have created. In *To Lie is Human* (Falcon Press), Dr. Christopher Hyatt writes, "Man is a powerful and joyous fool... He looks for power over himself and his environment. He is so creative—he invents ideas about himself and nature and bestows upon them an existence independent of himself..."

We engage this system quickly and often and then forget we have engaged it. We forget that we ourselves have created many of our own problems and limitations through internal representation and stories. We also forget that we have chosen to believe, accept and invest in the concepts thrust upon us by others. This is us pulling the wool over our own eyes—self-created phantoms that haunt us and "cause us" to suffer and ultimately fall far short of our potential.

> "We are all giants, raised by pygmies, who have learned to walk with a perpetual mental crouch."
> — Robert Anton Wilson

As you think on the above quote, realize that more often than not the mental crouch becomes a behavioral one as well. People *act out* the mental and emotional aspects. People do not make decisions or act solely based on logic. Regardless of the actual reality of the problem, we will respond more to our emotions—especially fear—than to facts. Our beliefs and fears, whether we are conscious of them or not, are the steering mechanism.

As we've discussed, words are *representations* of things, ideas and feelings. They are not the actual things, ideas and feelings. Words, stories and conclusions do not necessarily line up with reality. The same goes for your inner visualizations. You can imagine a purple gorilla with wings, a 10-foot spider or a talking sponge. The emotions your internal representations produce do not prove that these are real or valid, they just *seem* to do so. The gap between *seeming to* and *knowing for a fact that a threat or outcome is real and valid* is the difference between high-quality decisions and superstitions. Closing this gap is how many of your limitations are overcome.

I like to call what we have been looking at *The Veil of the Conceptual*. The ability to see through this veil, to walk through words, and to edit our internal map of meaning is our true power restored. Acknowledging the veil allows us to *come to choice* on how we respond to the world *and* our inner representation of it instead of robotically *reacting* to it.

Our ability to edit and update our internal map of meaning is within our *authority*. This means we can use our awareness and will to *author our own story* going forward, as well as to minimize the effect our past story has upon us now and in the future.

> **How much power can you (re)gain by seeing through the conceptual and thus making different decisions and conclusions?**

Limitation in Action

Consider the insidious downward spiral of self-limitation people commonly get themselves into. It starts with blaming their imaginary problems for causing their life issues. "I'm not successful because I'm not good enough" (the concept of metaphysical value politely and more commonly labeled as **low self-esteem**). This loops down further as the same imaginary problem becomes the excuse to avoid engaging in the behaviors that would address the life issue. "I don't feel that I can do those kinds of things because I'm not good enough." This shell game conveniently removes responsibility and power from the individual and places it upon the imaginary problem. Although this may alleviate some fear and anxiety in the short term, the downward spiral inevitably ends in failure and becomes self-fulfilling prophecy. The further down this spiral one goes, the less likely they are to recover.

Fortunately for us, a hole in our internal representational map does **not** mean that anything is missing in our reality. This gives us the *opportunity* to consider that some of our worst fears, insecurities and limitations are conceptual and therefore ***not real.*** What if the actual solution to these problems is not to *solve* them, but to stop believing in them?

Imaginary Problem 1: *I am no good, I am bad, I am not good enough.* This is also known as Metaphysical Value. We've talked about this a little already…and we are going to talk about it some more, because it is the single cause of most limitation, fear and psychological suffering.

Perceived Consequences: Abandonment, excommunication from the tribe, punishment, ceasing to exist, death.

The imaginary problem of ***not good enough*** is probably the most limiting of all and it is also the ultimate global generalization. It is taken to be factual and true in every context for all time—a final judgment of one's value or level of worth. Personal value is a metaphysical concept, and as such does not exist and cannot be measured. This imaginary problem is entirely reflexive and is based upon the *assertions* of other people. These assertions arise from other people's own personal agendas and tie into their religious and social *beliefs*. The general message is "You are ***no good*** if you are better than me, if you are different from me, if you don't agree with me, if you don't live up to my standards and if you in any way cause me to feel my own fears, insecurities and metaphysical value issues." This imaginary problem only exists because we have the language for it, meaning that it exists only in language.

The concept of one's metaphysical value is analogous to the M.C. Escher lithograph of the impossible object, *Ascending and Descending*, 1960:

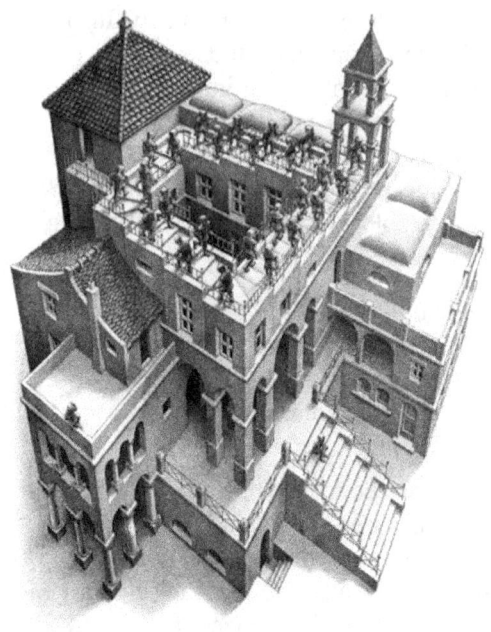

> **How can you climb higher and elevate yourself to *good enough* in that drawing?**

The problem cannot be fixed because it does not exist. The problem does not exist anymore than that staircase can be built in real life. Attempting to fix the problem only reinforces that the problem exists…much like searching for Bigfoot. This is a very deep idea and worth meditating on until it fully registers.

Imaginary Problem 2: *I can't.*

Perceived Consequences: Shame, embarrassment, failure, loss of status, punishment.

I can't implies perceived ability. Current ability is not a limit to what you are capable of, nor is it a measure of your "value." Success in any endeavor usually requires you to increase your ability. For example, if you are required to balance an income statement as a corporate accountant, or remove a gall bladder as a surgeon, then most likely you will need to increase your skill and ability in order to do

The Path to Personal Power

that properly. It takes ego strength to accept feedback and the implications of *not there yet* as you apply yourself to continual learning and development.

I can't also implies permission, as in ***I'm not allowed to*** or ***I'm not supposed to.*** It is the inculcation of the word NO. We hear this word many times in our lives; often born out of the fears of those who raised us. Rules for behavior in a specific time and context are generalized into future time and context and become systemic.

If you are honest with yourself, you will see that "I Can't" can usually be rephrased into "I'm afraid to."

Imaginary Problem 3: *It shouldn't be like this.*

Perceived Consequences: Pain, effort, anticipatory anxiety, disappointment, responsibility, work.

It shouldn't be like this quickly leads into the childish complaint *"I don't wanna have to!"* These are nothing more than complaints about reality not conforming to our wishes and whims—which are also concepts. Examples are: it's too hard; it takes too long; I don't feel like it; it should be more/less (add your favorite complaint here).

This imaginary problem often appears when we *think* or *feel* that we cannot operate successfully in the world *as it is* and *as we are.* Sometimes it is a byproduct of other imaginary problems such as *I'm not good enough* and *I can't.*

"I don't wanna have to" can easily lead to omitting information about future consequences. Be careful with the behaviors and decisions in your life that you think *don't count.* Children usually *don't wanna have to* brush their teeth. They either don't know or omit what it might be like to end up with a cavity or false teeth.

We all want things to be easy and come with a guarantee of success. We are all pain-avoidant to some degree. We all would like to return to the womb or find nirvana where all our needs and desires are instantly met. It would be nice *if we had been treated better* or *given what we needed (*or what we *thought* we needed). It would be nice if people could all get along and treat each other with respect. Unfortunately, life is often difficult, messy and unpredictable—especially when it comes to relationships with others. It takes ego strength to see and accept things as they are and to do something about it.

Your nervous system is attempting to steer you to stay in the tribe, and it can be very convincing. I encourage you to continuously re-evaluate your nervous system programming to determine if the signals it's sending you line up with reality, not just with your inner map.

> **Concepts influence your behavior.
> Your behavior mirrors the concepts you live by.**

To stop being limited by your conceptual problems, not only must you identify them, but you must also accept that on some level you believe in them. This can be difficult to see, as the process of creating concepts, accepting them as true, and forgetting you created them in the first place is not usually within our scope of awareness.

One thing that I have found incredibly helpful in finding your operational beliefs, concepts and conclusions is to *watch your behavior*. It is *MUCH* more effective to watch what you do, what you don't do, what you avoid, what you hesitate on and what you can't help yourself from doing or not doing than it is to listen to yourself *talk* about your beliefs. People can *say* just about anything, yet they cannot help but *act out* their beliefs and values, whether they are conscious of their true motivations or not.

It is important to think about your thinking and meditate on this until the understanding clicks into place for you. You have to drill all the way through the material for the understanding to be experienced. As you awaken to the un-reality of concepts, you will feel a sense of freedom. You are beginning to realize that you no longer need to remain in a self-created, self-limiting prison.

> **~ EXERCISE ~**
> Look at your life right now, where all of your limitations and problems are. Make a list of these.
> Make a separate list of the values and beliefs that you tell yourself and others you uphold.
> Reread the chapter.
> Compare this list to your actions, what you accomplish and what you avoid.

Chapter 15
Picking Up the Pieces

Q: What went wrong?
A: We were born as humans.

We humans punish ourselves for not being good enough. We decide when and if we are deserving of love. We mimic the behavior of the worst perpetrators upon ourselves in order to "be better" and "serve the ideals and concepts" that our perpetrators insist we agree with. We will do anything to stay in the tribe and to have an audience that agrees with the self-assigned labels we apply to ourselves. We do all of this unwittingly outside of consciousness, and then we wonder why we have no self-esteem or self-confidence. We wonder just who pushed us so far out of our integrity. We wonder why the achievement of certain goals is so difficult, and at times seems impossible. We wonder why happiness and fulfillment are so hard to reach, and why anxiety and depression come so easily and stay so long.

Most people are unaware of the function of their psychological and semantic black box. We are prisoners chained to the very thing that repeatedly shocks us and depletes our spirit, creativity and power. Shocks delivered in the hopes that we will overcome our shame, only support the erroneous belief in broken metaphysical value and add gasoline to the fires of our self-created inner hell. We will do almost anything to avoid the discomfort and infantile fears of being "bad" and the repercussions of "bad"—from loss of face to banishment from the tribe. Keep in mind that this happens whether you realize it consciously or not. Adults live "complex" lives that are nothing more than acting out *The Emperor's New Clothes,* living a story that does not exist. They live lives of quiet desperation, by accident, without knowing they are the **creators of their own nightmare**. Nobody is doing anything *to* you. The data you are taking in through your senses isn't doing anything *to* you. You are doing it all to yourself.

Most people are completely unaware of their conceptual inner fantasy world and how much it runs their lives. They never come to a decision on what concepts they are going to serve. They never get past the binary good/bad fictions and the labels they apply. They don't understand that labels and words and feelings do not add up to "truths."

They almost never question the existence (or lack) of the gods and the authorities (or their validity) that have made and continue to make decisions for them. They seldom get past their own superstitions.

It is difficult for an individual to learn about, digest and process these truths. It is painful to recall your developmental experiences and look at your shortcomings (more accurately stated as *improvement opportunities*). Look at all the ways people distract themselves from the truth. Look at how few people will engage in *short-term pain for long-term benefit*.

Remember that most never become aware of the idea that *feelings are proof,* which tells us that since it *feels* bad, it must *be* bad. Instead of facing inconvenient truths, we ignore them with self-righteous airs despite the fact that this painful work will improve our condition.

> **We desperately want someone to blame for all of this.**

On top of the odd neurology and developmental quirks, there are parents, teachers, religions, politics, police—virtually any form of authority—**who readily reinforce the game and use it to their own ends.** Keep in mind that, for the most part, the mechanism of the game—the black box—is unknown to even those who exploit it. They have merely figured out enough inputs and outputs to use it for their own ends. Be forewarned that there are a few who DO understand how to manipulate the game with the understanding that it is not real for *them,* **just real enough for you, to get you to behave the way they want you to.**

> **Authorities don't need to understand the black box to get you to do what they wish.**

The truth about what we really are has been outlawed because—get this—*it hurts people's feelings.* People will clamor and revolt if forced to realize their delusions, if forced to give up their entitlements. "It shouldn't be this way! Down with the (whatever the 'identified source' of their suffering)!" the angry mob cries.

Waking up causes personal and civil unrest. Social authorities don't need everyone questioning everything. For example, consider the War on Some Drugs that came shortly after the 1960's. The panic came from new pharmacology, primarily from research into psychedelics. At first the military thought they might be able to weaponize these drugs. Then, by accident, people figured out that mushrooms and LSD mimic the brain changes brought about by meditation and intense introspection. In other words, they caused people to question if they really wanted to play along in the consumer, political and religious games. That questioning did not serve the purposes of the authorities.

People will easily, quickly and violently oppose that which is "bad"—to avoid the discomfort, the difficulty and especially the labeling. ("You aren't a Nazi, are you?") Being a true believer and joining groupthink is *easy.* Plus, people don't like to go against the herd, as the herd will quickly label them as "bad" for not agreeing. ("You aren't *selfish,* are you?")

Few realize that our society is based on including everyone through the lowest common denominator. The more who are included, the more momentum the herd has. The closer the standards are to zero, the more people can join the herd, vote and pay up accordingly.

> **"Don't fool yourself, it's not survival of the fittest, it's survival of the *mostest!*"**
> **— Dr. Hyatt**

Social authorities exploit the inherent weaknesses and limitations of the human species whether they are conscious of it or not. Regardless, they gladly take your money in exchange for the illusion of safety and certainty and to relieve you of your responsibility.

There are those out there who are glad that you distract yourself from the truth. They are glad that you are a true believer and will rally around a cause, *any cause,* without looking to see who profits. This way your human nature can be used to forward *their* agenda while you collect labels and tell yourself how great you are, how much you are owed and how superior your beliefs are—the same beliefs that were fed to you by those who profit from them. We are sheltered from the truth for *our own good*. The baby is thrown out and the bathwater kept, sold back to them for a profit...while all along, unbeknownst to them, they are suffering the same asleep-at-the-wheel robotic fate. *Few in position of authority* are smart enough to understand this, communicate this and organize around it, let alone be able to keep quiet...so don't worry about conspiracies. **Unexamined human nature is the ultimate conspiracy.**

> **Few people have ever been exposed to this kind of thinking. I didn't create all of this...why isn't it taught at school? Why is it so hard to find?**

> **~ EXERCISE ~**
> Reread the words in the box above. Ask yourself a variation of Friedrich Nietzsche's question "Who benefits by this kind of thinking being so hard to find?"

Keep in mind that the most powerful of all the "rules" is not to question or go against authority. The absolute rule is to *obey*. This alone accounts for much of the historical justification for the *occult*, at least in terms of what needed to be kept *hidden*. Not long ago you could find yourself tortured and killed for questioning authority on "evil" matters such as looking through a telescope or declaring something idiotic, for instance that the earth revolves around the sun.

> **If you had the choice to wake up while having a nightmare, wouldn't you choose to stop it?**

Most humanimals never wake up to their human nature. They don't overcome themselves because they haven't been exposed to "why" they are and "how" to overcome it.

The fact that our neurological shortcomings are the effects of our development (programming)—whether nefarious, well-intended or accidental—can be a difficult pill to swallow. Few realize that the

The Path to Personal Power

human nervous system, coupled with the outcomes described in these chapters, create a feedback system. It is a system that mostly discourages true growth and creativity, and instead seeks to please the tribal authorities. It is as if one is fast asleep at the wheel of life…gas and brakes fully applied at the same time…high fiving ourselves while going nowhere and burning out the engine.

Yet, make no mistake that the true intent behind unmasking the neurotic monkey (humanimal) is **NOT** to make one feel bad and doom them to a painful and shameful life…but, rather, quite the opposite. The true intent is to set the monkey free and provide a path that builds personal power, self-reliance and success in multiple forms. Because without this, there is nothing more than self-deception and self-diminishment hiding behind the self-assigned labels of "special," "authentic" and "unique" while you look for the unicorn of unconditional love. Sometimes the monkey needs to be woken up by a swift kick in the seat!

Despite this gloomy perspective, the humanimal is *capable of* quite a bit of logic, thinking, creativity and acts of grace. Take special note in the idea of "is capable of," which does not mean that this happens as a matter of fact or all that often. Although the great traits that come from awakening and self-development are not all that common, they are indeed a possibility. The rarity of the great traits is why we celebrate them and strive towards them. *The decision to pursue this possibility is* **the true initiation.**

Self-evolution starts with waking the robot up.

Self-evolution and the power that comes with it carries a price, and that price is the removal of the mechanisms and props that comfort and coddle us during our nightmare. Example: Do you feel safest and most comfortable standing in the middle of the herd, and yet like to call yourself a "rebel"? I recall the "punk rockers" who thought of themselves as true rebels. They felt that they were excluded from society because they were different. They formed their own group with its own rules and dress codes, which ironically was even less accepting of difference than the society they were rebelling against. In their case the label and exclusivity was their prop, just the same as other groups in society.

Because these mechanisms and props make it easier to stay asleep, they will no longer be needed once the anxiety of the nightmare fades and we get on with living. True power does not need these props, and the sting of removing the blindfold that's over your eyes is better than the blindness and pain of perpetual stumbling it causes…even if doing so hurts your feelings for a bit.

> **Q: What is the solution to being born as a human?**
> **A: Waking up to your human nature, accepting it and working hard to overcome it.**

The Tipping Point

Chapter 16
Getting Out of Your Own Way

If there are some "most important" chapters to which I would have you pay special attention, the chapters in this section are it. If you are serious about doing the work, you will spend a lot of your time in this space. How much time? Enough time to be able to do the DOing that is described in the remaining chapters.

Our stated goal is to make yourself and your life into a work of art, while you work on waking up. To get more DOing done on both fronts, you must continue to get out of your own way. You must drop the excuses and break through the feelings of fear and guilt that hold you back.

You have the freedom and authority to live and build your life the way you want to. The work is about making the most of your freedom and the opportunity that you were presented with by being born.

> **Great Secret #7**
> You will spend the rest of your life working to get out of your own way…until you are out of your own way.

What are you waiting for?
What is stopping you?

Those are two very important questions. Think on these for a few moments and write your answers down before you read on.

Compare your answers to my answers below:

I don't know
I am waiting for something to stop or be taken away
I am waiting for something to start or be added

I am waiting for the right feelings to be present
I am waiting for the unpleasant feeling to be gone
I am waiting for permission
I am waiting to be good enough—to deserve it
Somebody else won't let me or doesn't want me to
I am waiting for someone else to help me or do it for me

I am waiting to feel better, to feel like it, for it to not have to be so hard. Oh, Those Previous Chapters! This real-life stuff leaves a mark and I just can't get past it. Or *can you*?

Remind me again... Who is the jailor and who is the prisoner?

If you have been paying attention, you may realize that...

> **Great Secret #11**
> There are no more NOWs that are *not* the right time to build and live your ideal life

There are no more present moments that are not the right time to get moving. Start taking steps NOW.

> **~ EXERCISE ~**
> Write down one thing you have been putting off that would make your life better. Get started on this today.

As you have been reading and experiencing what has been presented, you may begin to realize that there is no "higher" authority telling you what to do. It is you and your neurological programming that is holding you back. There is nobody above you on any spiritual ladder in control of your metaphysical value.

> **Look in the mirror at the great cosmic forces that are opposing you and thwarting your plans.**

It can be very hard to see that you are waiting for permission. You are waiting for it to be *"ok now"* to go about the things that you really want to be, have and do. You are waiting for a subtle feeling you have inside to dissipate. You "feel" it now and have felt it like a shadow behind you your whole life. This feeling is a phantom, a ghost that has haunted you more than you probably know or willingly admit. In fact, most people refuse to admit it and want to argue against it. I always get a kick out of how violently some people react to me telling them that everyone has a religion they hold true and follow. They holler about how they are "independent" and don't believe in God, organized religion, politics, whatever. What makes me so sure? I simply watch people *say* one thing and *do* another. I watch them worship their ghost and avoid their inner electric fence. Why else would a human being live out the statements "I want to, but I can't" and "I don't want to, but I have to"? Their true master is their neurological mechanism of control—their own nervous system—regardless of how it has been programmed. It is the ultimate authority. Perhaps it has been denied, ignored, externalized or deified up until this point. Now you need to *come to choice* on what you are going to do about it. You need to take responsibility for it. You need to start *DOing differently.*

> **You are held back by nothing more than your nervous system...and nervous it is!**

Your loyalty and fidelity have been to your programming. Getting out of your own way means that you need to go *against* your programming. You need to *rebel.* You must stop bringing your past forward. How? By DOing things that are self-enhancing whether your programming (learning) and your software (nervous system) *feel* that it's bad or not. You need to stop being a *follower* and start blazing your own trail. You need to stop operating within the guardrails and head in your own direction towards what it is that you truly are.

> **Be all that you can be. Be a *real* rebel.
> Rebel against your well-intentioned nervous system.
> Dare to change for your own benefit!**

Ancient man was superstitious...which means he put too much faith in his feelings, inklings and hunches. Without science, data and understanding he looked for "why" things happened in the stars, in the number 23, in the tribal stories like the Great Spider Grandmother or a flood that killed off the entire population of the world. Oh, sorry. Apparently, we aren't living in "advanced times"...yet.

What was the original sin? Not obeying the program(ming). Cast out of heaven, the great rebel fell...for doing his own thing. For not bowing down to the program(ming). Who does the programming serve? The *other*. Call it authority, god, mom, dad, teacher, preacher, policeman or even the "collective good." When your programming serves the *other*...AND...you go against it...OF COURSE you will be "labeled" as BAD.

> **When your programming serves the *OTHER*...AND...you go against it...OF COURSE you will be labeled as BAD.**

Man is in heaven when he is in harmony with himself *first* and then in integrity with others. In the stories, both man and the devil are cast out of a heaven and into hell for not putting himself second and for not prioritizing *others*. For not prioritizing others first every time and all the time, no matter what the cost.

(Before I get skewered for dissing religion...stop for a moment to consider that, if there is a supreme consciousness—a God—this wise entity must exist outside of the internal mental nonsense and nervous system mechanisms *in order to be, by definition, the supreme wise entity.* Any attempts to limit this infinite wisdom by comparing it to a human being and assigning it human characteristics—most of which are sub-optimal—would be insulting to it. Infinite wisdom would not bow down to its own mis-programmed nervous system, if it had one.)

Daring to put yourself first, to re-negotiate the rules of the game, is what it means to be Hyatt's *Psychopath*. This does not give license to act out your hate on others, hurt others or be a sociopath. It does not mean to *never* put others first. It takes power and discernment to live in the middle, away from the easy and lazy extremes.

Some will have you believe that you should NEVER be in the first spot on your list of priorities. The people who sell that are Hyatt's *Death-Worshippers*—who are anxiously waiting to get to the next life and are ok with sitting on the sidelines during this one. If you believe that you should *never* be first, then you do not fully value yourself or the opportunity to be alive. You think there will be another chance, that this is a dress rehearsal.

The Path to Personal Power

Why do people fall for this? They don't know better and it's easier than having to do the work presented here. They are cowards and would rather believe in fairy tales than take ownership of their life. They are busy dying while talking and labeling it something noble. They are collecting imaginary points for upholding their concepts.

> **YOU are the foundation your life is built upon.**

Dorothy was a great rebel in *The Wizard of Oz*. She helped her friends realize that by not being whole they were *selling themselves short*. This made them weak and ineffective until they realized that they did, in fact, have the traits needed within them, they had just hidden them from themselves—probably to appease others. She herself was afraid of witches, but it didn't stop her from eliminating them when they got in her way. She also courageously confronts the bad wizard—the "man behind the curtain"—for preying upon the fears and insecurities of others and using them for his own gain.

Please understand that all I've presented so far has been done so that you can free yourself. I'm just peeling back the curtain so you can get out of your own way.

The inscription on the Temple at Delphi should have read...

> **Know Thyself in order to get out of Thyself's own way!**

Chapter 17
Radical Acceptance

Radical Acceptance is the ability to look directly at yourself and the world and accept them as they are. This level of honesty both requires power and implies power. I find it amusing that the oft used quip "It is what it is" is actually a useful maxim to operate from.

Shit happens. It is unfortunate that you, at some point, are on the receiving end of some *shit happening.* Your parents were amateurs without proper training and made mistakes that you were the recipient of. Your nervous system develops in a less-than-optimum way. You have had rejection of some form and probably have experienced a flat tire, bee sting, shit your pants and missed out on something due to the weather. One big shortcut in life is accepting what is and getting on to *what's next* instead of resisting life as it unfolds.

People resist accepting life, often very violently and petulantly. *Shit happening* against their wishes and plan is a direct affront to their ego. But we don't want to support an ego; *we want to support your authentic self and your potential.*

There is much that you do not wish to be true of you, or of the world around you. And as you know from experience, wishing is not an effective strategy—it is a waste of energy. Saying "no" to your reality is nothing more than a childish protest.

Get Over Yourself

Putting the weight of your mistakes and shortcomings onto your sense of self is a mistake. You must come to terms with and accept the fact you aren't as good as you *think* you are. You aren't perfect, so you work to have enough personal power to admit this and continue on with making yourself and your life into a work of art.

The Path to Personal Power

> You aren't perfect.
> Shit happens.
> AND
> You **get to** say...
> Who Cares?

You *can* say "Who cares?" can't you? The recovery from *shit happening* is a simple process:

Step 1) **"So What?"** At face value this can seem to be an insensitive and insulting question...but it is not. There is an answer. After some shit happens to you, you might feel angry, frustrated, betrayed, depressed or a combination of things. It is important to *accept* how you feel. Maybe you feel like quitting, pouting and having a self-pity party. Great, that is your SO WHAT! I hear you loud and clear and empathize with you. You didn't sign up for that *shit happening* and you are hurt, frustrated, angry and scared.

Step 2) **"Now What?"** Best not to start with step 2. Most people do because they have trouble sitting with the feelings in step 1. Life can create some real anguish and suffering. Let people have their step 1. Let *yourself* have your step 1. If you look back over your own experience, you will find that at some point you got past step 1. You cried it out, kicked and screamed and eventually it subsided. Maybe you got bored. Then you moved to *"Now What?"* and took the next steps. You got a flat tire, swore and punched the steering wheel, took some breaths, complained to whomever would listen...and now you are on the phone with the tow truck. You get it fixed, write a check and have a strong bourbon later on.

Step 3) **Wash, Rinse and Repeat**. Forever this will be your strategy, as life will continue to present you with more *shit happening*.

Tips: The faster you can get through this process while supporting yourself, the better. It is a skill that can be developed. Some people call this "having a thick skin." The more careful you are with your *chosen response* (not robotic violent reaction) the less damage you do from a place of weakness and emotionality. Doing less damage from an emotional place is good to practice as it saves much time and resources. Why let one problem spiral into many? You don't really need to, nor can you justify lighting your car on fire because it got a flat tire.

Radical Acceptance is the powerful path through life, and with it you learn to cope with the shit in life, even thriving in it. Some people refuse to accept what happens, and this insistence on being the victim places a great weight upon their spirit. If this attitude and direction is left unchecked, it soon begins to weaken your spirit and will eventually crush it beyond repair. This is having contempt for yourself and your life due to the fact that it isn't perfect, it isn't easy, and you just don't get your way every single time. Those who fall down and promise themselves they will not get up are playing a very dangerous game. It doesn't take long to lose your way in that darkness and never again emerge from it. Attempting to punish others and the world for the slights you have taken and attempting to spread your poison onto them is a fool's game. It only deepens your belief in your own weakness and bolsters your lack of value and deservingness.

It is one thing to hit bottom and wake up from the jolt. It is another thing to hit bottom, refuse to get up and attempt to harm those who would help you up.

Radical Acceptance requires you to learn how to be nice to yourself. Being hard on yourself and punishing yourself is mostly just introjected bad parents and other authority figures. Do you talk to yourself in a harsh and judgmental way? Do you shame yourself and tell yourself you aren't worthy? This didn't help when you were little—when others did this to you—and it's not helping now as you do it to yourself.

> You get to choose how to manage yourself, so you might as well choose to treat yourself in a way that promotes the development of your power and potential.

Great Secret #43
You get to choose how you *respond* to life.
You don't *have to*…you GET TO respond powerfully.
There is great freedom in this.

The Path to Personal Power

Many of my clients complain bitterly about how their parents and others treated and continue to treat them…while using the same internal dialogue on themselves. If this is true of you, then it's time to start being a proper parent (authority) to yourself. One power that a judge (or parent) has is to *pardon*. Are you not your own judge yet? Lighten up on yourself. No good will come from being mean to yourself. Learn to see how you are doing this, and then *stop it.*

Leave yourself alone. Who is it that is setting up the judgment? Who is the "eye in the sky"? We forget that *we* internally conceptualize this, and then we are guilty, judged and shamed by ourselves. In fact, even if others judge and shame us, it is *our agreement* with them that is what makes it our personal reality, not their judgment.

Radical Acceptance requires you to accept the world as it is, and not waste energy complaining and feeling sorry for yourself because the world doesn't work the way you would like it to. Gravity, hard work, odd people, randomness, death and taxes are among the facts of life that we would like to change. You can learn much about yourself by noting which aspects of the world you dislike the most. For example, if you are violently opposed to bullying, it may indicate your dislike of your own bottom-dog life script, past events in your life, or both. It is best to equip yourself with the strength and skills to deal with the difficult situations in life. Complaining and protesting usually do nothing but boost your negative feelings and delay the inevitable: taking responsibility for your life outcomes.

One important fact of life to understand is the idea of *tabula rasa,* or the psychological "clean slate." There are many therapies, groups, self-help and new age movements (and salesmen) that romanticize the idea that one day you will be totally FREE. Once you have some enlightenment experiences, take the special training, stop saying "no" to the universe or buy the product, you will no longer suffer or feel fear and anxiety. While it is true that by doing the work we have been discussing in this book, fear and suffering will decrease and joy, relaxation, creativity and achievement will increase—but it often takes a while.

Start to notice how much the concept of the "destination" has been programmed into your thinking. The destination promises a "happy ever after" similar to the clean slate. Once you reach your destination, there will be more work to do and more places to go. Marriage is a great example of this. We are shown from a young age how we will ride off into the clouds once we are in love and married. Real life shows us that banking on this to happen on its own is part of the reason for such high marital failure rates. The truth is that relationships take deliberate thoughtfulness, hard work and plenty of getting out of your own way. If you are prepared to apply the best of yourself and commit to hard work at all stops on your journey and in between, you open up the option of being outstanding the whole way.

> Don't hesitate and wait for the clean slate.
> Sometimes it takes a lot of scrubbing.
> Might as well be building your ideal life
> while your slate is at the cleaners.

This path reminds you that sometimes there is not going to be a clean slate any time soon. You are going to have to not only ***accept*** fear, anxiety and discomfort—you are going to have to push through them and ***do the right things anyway.*** What kind of person needs a clean slate and a guarantee before they will commit to themselves or a course of disciplined action? One who does not have the will, skill, stomach or power to make it happen despite their current reality. Sometimes learning and healing happen on the first try, which is always welcome. Often it takes many repetitions and much effort. Some aspects of yourself will change more quickly and easily than others. Either way, if you value yourself and chose to work towards your own ends *enough,* you will see it through. If you *choose* to not see it through, then power and mastery will continue to elude you.

> **"But anything is possible!"**

This mantra is often the battle cry of those who do not want to face their fears and do what is required. Holding out hope for a "miracle," for the "ultimate" cure, process, answer or guarantee is a flight from the nature of life. This person is waiting for other people to change, circumstances to become easier, and fears to disappear because life doesn't suit him. It is another way of saying you would actually start *DOing* something…if the terms and conditions of life were different.

> **Do it RIGHT anyway. Start NOW.**

Too many people fail in silent protest about the way things are instead of getting over themselves and learning to win. You must push through life and *Do it RIGHT anyway.* You don't feel the way you want to? *Do it RIGHT anyway.* It takes more effort, time and persistence than you "thought" it would? *Do it RIGHT anyway.* You can use your child-like (and child-formed) preconceptions and expectations as a standard of evaluation, complain and wish life was different…or you can *Do it RIGHT anyway* and get results.

What is Radical Acceptance?

Accepting the randomness of life…
Accepting that you've lost some battles…
Accepting human developmental limitations…
Accepting your past…
Accepting the rules of the game…
Accepting that you think you are "owed" something…
Accepting that things take more work than you think…
Accepting that you are afraid and anxious…
Accepting that you have programming to overcome…
Accepting that you have qualities you try to hide and disown…
Accepting that it is up to you alone to do something about yourself…
Accepting that nobody cares more about you than you do…

You cannot move from anyplace other than from where you *actually* are. You may not like where you are or how you got there, but you need to know where you currently are. You can only move forward from *here* and *now*.

Chapter 18
Therapy(ies)

Defining therapy is difficult without defining the end goal. If you do some research on the question of "What is the purpose of therapy?" you get a wide variety of results. Common among these are to provide a safe place to talk about your problems, thoughts and feelings; or to become the healthiest version of yourself and to lead a happy, healthy, productive life. On the surface these do not sound too bad.

The goal of therapy should be in line with the goals of the individual. It is important to acknowledge *Primum non nocere,* which is Latin for "First, do no harm." This principle is taught to remind practitioners that it is good to consider whether or not a course of action may do more harm than good. The material in this book is presented with the assumption that the reader is of sound mind and body to absorb them. If you feel that you may not be ready for these ideas, then feel free to dismiss them.

There are many individuals who need to address different and more serious psychological and neurological issues, and this may preclude them from doing what I am presenting here. Major depression, bipolar disorders, schizophrenia, severe personality disorders, drug addiction and other neurological conditions require psychological and often medical treatment. These populations are not the intended audience for this book as they are much different from what is called the "worried well." The "worried well" are people who have the ability to progress much further than they "feel" or "think" that they can, and it is these people that constitute the audience I am addressing. While it may be very beneficial to tell someone in the "worried well" group to get over themselves and get on with it, this would not be a kind or useful message for someone who has more serious issues, as they are most often **not** at choice about those issues.

Many people pursue therapy because they do not like how they feel most of the time. They are unhappy, don't like themselves, feel stuck,

The Path to Personal Power

or all of these. They are frustrated with life, with other people in their life, and with their lack of progress. They are afraid they aren't good enough, afraid they will fail, and lack the confidence to engage in the behaviors required for success and building a great life. These are valid reasons to pursue therapy, yet the desire to fully maximize your potential and to come to know who you truly are and what you are capable of is a much stronger motivation and a necessary key to doing the work as it is presented in this book. You need to want to do more than just relieve temporary unhappiness.

> The purpose of therapy in the context of this book is to help you get to a place where you are ready, willing and able to "Do all of the DOing" necessary to create yourself and your life into your own self-styled word of art.

Feeling better is a "normal" and reasonable outcome, but it is not the destination. Once you *feel better…then what?* Do you need to feel *completely* better to start making changes in your life? The Work is seldom tailored to what people *think* and *feel* they need. The goal of the Work is to create yourself and your life into a work of art while working on waking up. Thus, the nature of the work in all its facets is going to go deeper and further than "normal" to create something that is more grand and ultimately more valuable and enjoyable than what "normal" seeks.

The Work puts pressure on each individual, similar to the feeling you get standing on the end of a diving board for the first time. The goal is to get into the water headfirst, not to remove all fear. It is natural to feel conflict between the goal and fear. Learning to get past fear, not getting rid of it, is the key to success. Seeking to eliminate fear is a distraction that makes fear the excuse to not be *doing*. A more reasonable goal is to learn to adequately cope with the pressures of life and make decisions that are backed up by actions to propel you forward—often regardless of how you feel.

It is powerful to insert a philosophical component into therapy, as philosophy seeks to answer the question, "How should we then live?" This depends on the goal of therapy. My view is that the goal should be to maximize your human potential. That is a high bar to clear, and requires much different work than the common goal of therapy, which is to put a Band Aid on the psychological boo-boos and get the client plugged back into society.

> Apparently, this entire book has something to do with therapy, although deeper and more inclusive than most therapy.

Much of the Work has a therapeutic effect as the actions and principles point in the direction of a healthy and powerful individual. In many disciplines of personal advancement, you will cross therapeutic bridges and come face to face with the erroneous beliefs, fears and demons that seem to get in your way. Whether therapy *needs* to be its own endeavor really depends on the individual and the amount of progress he is making *in real life*.

Common therapy leads to better feeling and better thinking. For our purposes, we need to take this a step further and *agree* that it leads to more DOing in the real world. Therapists are not chartered to be the accountability police as that would put pressure on the client which may, in turn, make them feel bad, regress and/or remove the safe element of the therapeutic space.

Sometimes therapists and clients get stuck in the rut of letting therapy be an end in itself. This provides steady income for therapists and an excuse to stay sheltered for clients. The purpose of therapy and personal philosophy is to help you to build a solid foundation on which to build your life. Without that foundation, life can be scary and overly difficult. Yet by building *only* a foundation, you aren't getting around to building a life *on top of* that foundation.

The most effective way to look at therapy is to do it, apply it to yourself, and then go out in the real world and put yourself out there. Build new skills, make progress, find out where you get stuck and what fears get in your way; then bring that information back to the therapy space. You can do this with a teacher/mentor/therapist, on your own, or both. You can utilize "therapeutic" topics, all the information you gather from this and other books, as well as your experience and feedback from life itself. This attitude prevents you from becoming a therapy junky and teachers and therapists from becoming pushers. Pushers want clients who are addicted for life. Real teachers want students to fly powerfully on their own as soon as possible.

Chapter 19
Measuring Progress

> **Great Secret #3**
> "Everything Counts in Large Amounts"
> — Depeche Mode

People are measuring themselves, measuring others and making comparisons to standards and to each other all the time. Without measurement and feedback, it is very difficult to know where you are—which you need to make adjustments and gauge progress.

Measurement is necessary to produce quality. If you are cutting wood to frame a house, you don't just guess. Too many people guess at important things in life.

Often measuring is labeled as "judging" and thus avoided because most people do not like feedback. Most have difficulty separating a specific measurement from their ego. They are afraid they will not "measure up." Regardless of how you look at it, measuring and comparing happens all the time whether we admit it or not. As this is the case, we will make use of it and learn to do it well. Here are some excellent ways to measure progress.

Direct Measurement

The best and most obvious way to measure progress is directly. If you are a runner, and your event is the 10k, then you can time yourself. As you train and compete you measure your progress by your event times.

As you progress in the work, you should not only be able to *say* you are better than average, but *measure* that way as well. As this is being written the estimated U.S. population is 325 million. Do you know the median income, body fat percentage, life savings, debt and education levels for someone your age? If you work at those facets of your life, you should expect to become better than "average."

Not everything is easy to measure. Financial success falls prey to relativity. Statistical norms based on your career might help, as will financial literacy and familiarity with investments. Progress in your career is based on your level of skill, quality of work, quality of relationships, your network, and, sometimes, luck. When you have to rely on *reasonable measures* of progress, the rest of this chapter will be useful.

In terms of looking at your overall progress, you will need to determine what is important to you and how you define success and fulfillment. You cannot be a master at everything, and there is not a universal measure of success. The following chapter addresses this.

Feedback

A great predictor of future success and power is how well you accept constructive feedback. This is a master skill in life, and your rate of progress is highly correlated to your ability to seek out and accept feedback. Feedback helps you to increase the accuracy and effectiveness in what you do.

People who take feedback well:

> Take responsibility for their actions
> Take ownership of their results or lack of them
> See feedback as a gift that helps them improve
> Develop a thick skin
> Are more prone to see life objectively
> Actively seek out feedback
> Suffer less and accomplish more
> Learn faster
> Are seen as coachable and teachable
> Are seen as trustworthy
> Are seen as loyal and caring

People who do not take feedback well:

> Blame others for shortcomings
> Tend to have a lot of excuses

The Path to Personal Power

- See feedback as mean punishment
- See life as unfair
- Have thin skin and give up easily
- Avoid and resist feedback opportunities
- Are seen as emotionally volatile and high maintenance
- Are considered less trustworthy and less dependable
- Are seen as less coachable and promotable
- Tend to be set in their ways instead of learning new tricks

The good news is that processing feedback is a skill that can be learned and improved upon. Most people do not start out being good at it because they take it personally. They feel as though the feedback is rating more than it actually is—like their entire self-worth. For example, not being good at math does not mean that you are stupid. Math is not the only measure for being smart and having potential.

The key to measuring progress and feedback is to not take it personally. I'm sure you have heard this many times before. The *way* to do this is to keep feedback and measurement around specific skills and progress and *not* around your personal value. This is a distinction *you yourself* need to make and enforce. Feedback is not the measuring of your worthwhileness as a human being (metaphysical value). Metaphysical value is a trap. It is a cheap way to gain compliance over someone (especially a child who cannot discern this game). This has happened to you and it has happened to everybody. Determine to let it go and get past it.

Leave yourself alone in this manner. Leave your personal value, self-worth, self-esteem or what-have-you out of it. Leave it alone and focus on the skills and tasks at hand. How much feedback hurts your feelings and how much you take personally is a good measure of progress in-and-of-itself. It is up to you alone to do this. Remind yourself at all times to not take it personally and look at feedback as an opportunity to improve.

Sometimes feedback comes in the form of judgement, is harsh or the intent is to harm instead of help. These reasons don't necessarily make the feedback untrue, just unpleasant. When this happens, drop the judgmental, violent and punitive part. It is not the other person who is hurting you, **it is your agreement with them that hurts you**. There is an old saying that even a broken clock is right twice a day. In these situations, sift out anything useful that you can own and improve and discard the rest. This way, even jabs that were meant to slow you down or discourage you make you stronger.

> It is not the other person's words that hurt you, it is your ***agreement*** with them that is the problem.

You do not need the permission of others to make mistakes. You do not need the blessing of others to be a continually learning and improving machine. You need permission from yourself to be "not quite there yet" and to get on with it. The other option is to feel sorry for yourself and to be against yourself while blaming others and the cruel, difficult world for your shortcomings.

Most people are conditioned to think of feedback as negative and hurtful. You can learn to see feedback as something generative for you by digging a little deeper into it. Consider a *negative feedback loop*. Negative feedback loops work to bring a process *back towards equilibrium*. This loop is designed to take measurements in order to self-correct with a given constraint. An example of this is a thermostat. It measures the air temperature and then either cools or heats the air *to keep it within a certain range* and prevent the home from getting too hot or too cold. This has a corrective connotation.

On the other hand, a *positive feedback loop* tends to accelerate a system *away from equilibrium*. An example is receiving praise for good performance, which leads to greater efforts in performance and thus more praise. The important point is that performance is not supposed to revolve around *status quo,* but is to be continually improving.

A *feed-forward mechanism* is designed to use a measurement and then direct behavior towards a future ideal state. It provides options that are more often seen as improvements to technique and process with the goal of improving effectiveness.

It is good practice to interpret feedback that you receive in the frame of feed-forward—that the feedback, or parts of it, can be used to steer you to greater effectiveness…**regardless of the tone or intentions** of the giver. By controlling your own interpretation, you will avoid shifting into the negative thought loop of "I'm no good" (metaphysical value again). It is also quite effective to use the feedforward frame when giving feedback to others.

> Yes, I keep bringing *Metaphysical Value* up, because I want you to fully let it go.

Mastery *Inferred*

The definition of inference: drawing a conclusion based on information you have.

Think of a garden. Imagine that in this garden there are many varieties of rare and beautiful plants and flowers. They are laid out in a way that brings out the contrast of their colors and shapes. The garden was carefully planned to make use of their different heights, colors and blooming schedules. This garden is meticulously cared for. The plants are trimmed, the soil is weeded and the rocks are placed in a deliberate way to accentuate its features. The babbling brook and small pond are clean and clear and host beautiful small fish.

Now imagine a second garden. This one is overgrown with weeds and hasn't been attended to in a while. Some of the plants are overgrown and choking out the others, while others have browned and died. Over in the corner you spot some garbage that the wind blew in. The brook is almost dry and covered in algae and brown slime. The pond is stagnant and smells of dead fish, which can be seen floating on top.

> You are the garden.

The information you have at hand is that gardens do not grow on their own. Gardens do not organize themselves in nature. They take planning and hard work. Although the second garden is in disrepair, there is still an opportunity to straighten it out.

In comparing the two gardens, what might you infer about how important they are to the gardener? In the first instance, you would think that the garden is loved and cared for. It must be a source of beauty, joy and pride. On the other hand, the other garden is neglected and uncared for. It must not be important. Maybe it's not special or valuable. In either case, the gardens are a reflection of the gardener.

> You are also the gardener.

Would you go to a grossly overweight physical trainer? Would you go to a yoga teacher who couldn't touch his toes? Would you eat at a restaurant that was always empty, smelled funny and has a lot of flies?

Take a look at yourself and your life. You, as well as others, are drawing inferences and attaching meaning about your personal state of affairs. Since *you* are watching, it makes sense to behave in a way that shows care and love for yourself. If you do not take care of yourself and your life, you will feel shame and embarrassment.

> Since **YOU** are always watching, you might consider abstaining from thoughts, speech and behavior that does not hold yourself in high regard…
> just in case you might believe yourself.

What comes to mind as you read the following questions?

- Do you bathe regularly?
- Do you maintain your hair?
- Do you cut and trim finger nails and toenails, no dirt and schmutz under them?
- Do you maintain a healthy bodyweight?
- Do you exercise and strengthen your body?
- Do you stretch and maintain flexibility?
- Do you eat in a way that provides nourishment for your body?
- Do you brush and floss your teeth?
- Do you wash your clothes and dress well?
- Are you constantly learning new things?
- Is your home clean and organized? Is it in good repair?
- Is your fridge clean, or is it a science project in there?
- Is your car clean and well maintained, or could it support a homeless family for a week?
- Are your personal finances in order? Are you in debt or investing for your future?
- Do you have a network of peers and professionals who support you and your goals?

The Path to Personal Power

There are many more items that could be put on this list. Each of these little things adds up and makes a difference in how you see yourself and how others see you. What looks like mastery? What looks like failure?

> You are your life are your own best investment. Take care of it.

People tend to rate themselves quite favorably. This is called being *a legend in your own mind*. This may help the sensitive ego feel good, but it is a hindrance to real development and progress. If we think we are halfway there, and we are only 10% there, then we are going to think the bar is a lot lower than it really is. In reality, the bar is always a bit *higher* than we think it is. This often comes as a shock and can discourage people. Instead, look at the hidden benefit of this—when you DO clear the bar, the victory and value of it is all the greater.

People who strive towards personal power and self-mastery do so through their actions. Many of their successful actions lead to results. When you look at your life, at what you touch and your trail of results, are you finding evidence of victories?

> **Great Secret #2**
> People will say anything to themselves and others, yet have a very difficult time *not* acting out their values. Measure actions and results, not words and "beliefs."

Self-Enhancing or Self-Diminishing

The continuum of Self-enhancing to Self-diminishing is one of my absolute favorite tools. It is very simple. It cuts through the guff and is almost impossible to argue with. All you need to do is ask yourself (or others) the simple question, "Is doing X self-enhancing or self-diminishing?"

Is it self-enhancing to brush and floss your teeth? Of course it is. How about getting enough sleep? Yes. What about being very hard on yourself and criticizing yourself for not being perfect? Hmmm, let's see. This patterned response to life seems to cause anxiety and depression. Neither of these emotional states cohabitate with creativity, productivity or love. Apparently, this self-communication strategy is self-diminishing. Interestingly enough, when this was done to you as a child *you felt it was self-diminishing!* Then why keep doing it? Are you a robot?

The goal is to change the ratio of self-enhancing behaviors to self-diminishing behaviors, so that over time you spend more of your time and energy doing that which is self-enhancing not self-diminishing. This is the single best measurement for success (if it could be measured) that I have found.

Looking at how you spend your time is a great gauge. Keep track of the ratio of how much time you spend each day doing self-enhancing and self-diminishing behaviors. See how this affects your mood and your results in life. Momentum can easily be created and increased this way.

You may find yourself *knowing* what would be a great use of your time and energy and then *doing* something else, like surfing the web or watching tv. You may find yourself having a lot of "good intentions" and then doing all of the least important things first, running out of time to do what is really important and self-enhancing. By paying attention and documenting these cases you will learn a lot about yourself. You can use this knowledge to uncover fears and beliefs. The places you tend to get stuck are ripe opportunities to improve, heal and overcome limitations.

Using this tool requires common sense. Getting a good night's sleep is self-enhancing, while sleeping all day usually is not. Certain drugs are helpful in context, but used habitually as a lifestyle may become self-diminishing and possibly self-extinguishing. If you find yourself arguing with the concept, check to see if you have an overactive "label" at work in your mind. "Rebel," "Eco Warrior," "Martyr" and just about any over-used platitude or cause-of-the-month can get you believing there is merit to self-diminishing behavior.

How You Spend Your Time

How you spend your time is a good measure of self-esteem. Is it spent self-enhancing? Pay attention to what you actually *do*. People will say anything, but they always act out their values. You may find you are serving *old programming* instead of your own values.

What happens when you know that what you are doing is self-diminishing and you do it anyway? You are out of integrity with yourself, which produces stress, guilt and shame. This behavior will also highlight conflicting values. You may value both relaxation and productivity, do too much of one or switch from extreme to extreme. In that case, avoiding extremes is more self-enhancing.

You may have been programmed to feel guilty when you do nice things for yourself because your parents were too full of guilt to enjoy life and needed to keep you from "getting too big of a head on your shoulders." Now when you do something self-enhancing, you have an unnatural and negative emotional response. It is self-enhancing to work to reprogram this. It is self-enhancing to do it anyway.

It is self-enhancing to improve yourself and your life regardless of how you "feel." This is another way to look at "discipline." You are being a disciple of your best self, not being punished to work as a slave. Arguing against the idea of self-enhancing is only stating that you "would rather not have to" change.

Overall, as you progress down this path, you should expect to notice general improvements in your mood. You should have more free time, more space and more energy to be creative and engage in self-enhancing behaviors.

You are looking to reduce stress, suffering, anxiety and guilt. You are looking to increase joy, peace, strength, flexibility, relationships, resources and wealth.

> ***Get over yourself*** and get busy creating yourself and your life into a work of art.

Chapter 20
What Do You Want?

What do you want in your life? You may find this question difficult to answer. You might draw a blank, you might have some loose ideas. On the other hand, you might be very specific about the answer. If you don't know, it's your job to find out.

> Q: How do I get to where I'm going?
> A: I don't know. It depends on where you are going.

It is surprising how many people really don't know how to answer the question of what they want.

We have defined the goal of the work as making yourself and your life into your own self-styled work of art—while working on waking up. One of your most important developmental tasks is to decide what it is that you want. It is your responsibility to figure this out. I strongly suggest that you remain true to yourself and not look to others to tell you. If you don't figure it out, there are plenty of people who will be happy to put you to work doing what *they* want.

Why don't people know what they want? Do they know but are afraid to admit it? Why? It may be that they are perfectionists, want a guarantee, or are trying to not-screw-it-up. Some people believe deep down that they can't be wrong or judged if they do nothing. Keep in mind that is only true in the short term. Most people who play it safe end up with very unremarkable lives. Does labeling this life "not-losing" make it winning?

I get a lot of calls from people who know me through someone in the career counseling realm. It's not my area of specialty, but I get positive feedback around the questions I ask people to think on:
- What would you enjoy doing all day long?
- What are you so passionate about that you might put in the effort to be the best in the world at it?

The Path to Personal Power

- Is there a career that would seem like playing to you? Something you would do without a lot of pay?
- How do you spend your free time? What are you drawn to? What do you admire?
- What really bothers you? What would you like to eliminate for yourself and others?
- What kind of people do you like to be around? How many and for how long?

These questions easily translate from your career to your whole life. If you look at your other likes, wants, needs and preferences, you can sketch out your life.

Look at the stereo equalizer as a metaphor. Each slider on this component relates to a sonic frequency. By adjusting these up and down you can boost or cut certain frequencies. A large room may need more bass, certain speakers may need extra highs added in or you may prefer a certain musical *balance*.

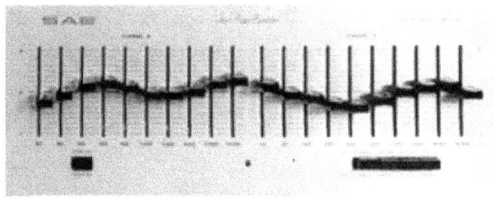

Consider labeling each slider for something that you value: money, travel, luxury, adventure, free time, mind, body, etc. Some of these may contraindicate others, such as money and free time or health and luxury. It might be unrealistic to increase these at the same time. The goal is to adjust these until your life has the right *balance* for you.

Keep in mind that if you push all the sliders to the top, you basically do nothing besides making the music louder—which eliminates the point of the component (or, in our case, the metaphor) completely.

Caveats

If you have trouble with knowing and deciding what you want, you need to learn to trust your instincts. You develop this trust through **repetition.** By making decisions and checking the outcomes, you get *data*. The more decisions, the more data and hence the better you get at the process.

How *other people* respond to your choices is tricky data, and not the only data. You should strive to improve your life and well-being without lowering that of others. At times others may be offended by *any* amount of *your* improvement. This can become important data for you in terms of the kind of people you want in your life, but not data in terms of what is good for you to be doing.

Another important and related caveat is that your goals shouldn't be to solve your problems of metaphysical value—how good you are, how deserving and how likable you are. It is related because these judgments primarily start with "other" people and what is good for *them*. Having a lot of money won't change this, so becoming a lawyer for that reason will be a long life unless you enjoy doing that work.

If you see "destination" thinking pop up, this is a good indicator that you are trying to fix something. "Someday when I finally (get something, get rid of something) then I will be (happy, fulfilled, free, etc.)" There is no one thing that will fix you. There are no *external* things that will fix you. You will be "all better" when you *decide* that you are. If you put the weight of your healing and development on destinations and externals, you will be disappointed.

Doing

Chapter 21
From "Knowing Of" to Knowing

There is a saying: "Nothing wins like winning," and for the student of power this is an essential fact of life. The most effective method of gaining power is *DOing*. Direct action in the world—practice and incorporating feedback while adjusting as you go—is the most direct route. In fact, nothing can take the place of direct experience.

This brings us directly to an important distinction: between "knowing" and "knowing of." Most people will readily substitute "knowing of" for real knowledge and results. Everyone is an expert on the state of affairs on a certain subject after watching a *60 Minutes* exposé or documentary. Yet you cannot *know* skydiving until you have jumped from a plane. Reading book after book on marksmanship will only do so much for hitting the bullseye, yet it might make you *appear* to be proficient at the garden party.

A master never substitutes *knowing of* for direct knowledge and experience, because he would rather have real results than talk about theories and parrot what he has read. Real results are infinitely more valuable than "book smarts" (or television or internet) as they increase momentum and power. Armchair quarterbacks are common and therefore worthless. People who can get things done are rare.

"Knowing of" provides two functions. First it allows us to convince ourselves that we "know" and thus do not need to actually experience the work behind it. Everyone loves a good movie montage where you become a ninja and learn to fight with all the weapons, become extremely strong and capable…all in about 3 minutes.

People do not like to be measured and hate the feeling on wobbling and being "not there yet." Children, when fantasizing about being an adult, sports hero or superhero do not pretend to be the 3rd string baseball player who only is allowed on the field when the team is up by ten runs.

Second "knowing of" allows us to increase our status around other people because we are "in the know." Many people would rather win a debate with their *opinion* rather than get real results through hard work.

The downside of "knowing of" is that it is a false representation of yourself and your abilities. You will be found out by those who *do* know because your results will not match your claims, and your misrepresentation will have the opposite effect you originally hoped for. It will weaken you and your position with those who have more power. There is a part of you that knows you are lying to yourself, which in-and-of-itself makes you weak and implies that your low standards and pretending are good enough. If it happens that you aren't found out, then you can be sure you aren't in the same circles as those who are wise enough to know the difference.

> **~ EXERCISE ~**
> Pay attention to how often you tell people what you "know" yet haven't DONE. Make a list of the topics you do this with.

The most important subject on which you can use the distinction between knowing of and knowing is *yourself.* Coming into this work, most people only *know of* their own power. They are hopeful that they will come to know it. Often, they have read about or seen it in others. Obtaining the power of self-knowledge and the results it brings is the subject of the archetypal hero's journey. Thus, people come to the work with many ideas, notions and conclusions as to what the work is about, how to go about it and what works the best, when most times they haven't done enough to know. A common example is the kid who grew up in a very religious household and finally gets out of the house. He starts reading fringe and occult authors, feels that he knows the way to freedom, and starts simultaneously doing psychedelics and advanced meditation techniques. He soon finds himself anxious and depressed, if not in a serious psychological condition, haunted by fears and guilt around what he has done to his family and religion. He hasn't done any real psychological work (or work in the external world) and therefore has no solid foundation to build on. Assembling a strategy by picking and choosing what suits you without knowing better is a recipe for trouble.

> Q: How do you get to "knowing" from "knowing of"?
> A: By **DOing**

Chapter 22
DOing

This may seem blatantly obvious, but to make yourself and your life into your work of art, you have to **DO** things. Many people are waiting around to start doing the things that bring them the results they want in their lives.

> What are **YOU** waiting for?

Refer back to your answers from the chapter *Getting Out of Your Own Way*. To refresh your memory, here are my favorite answers.

Waiting for permission
Waiting to feel good or not feel bad
Waiting until you can see every step
Waiting for a guarantee that it will work out
Waiting for other people to join in; not having to be alone
Needing to be perfect and/or right

> Remember...there is no time that is not the right time to be doing something self-enhancing.

Most of these are excuses to keep yourself from feeling discomfort and/or to excessively please other people. You are going to have to face your feelings at some point, so stop putting things off.

If one of your goals is to dive from a diving board, then at some point you will have to face the first dive. There is an old Zen saying, "If not now, when?" This means that whether your first dive is in two minutes, or you put it off for two years, it will still be your first dive. What you will feel will be what you will feel, and delaying DOing won't change the feeling significantly enough to make not-doing self-enhancing. If it takes 1,000 dives off the board for you to reach your level of mastery, then the sooner you start, the sooner you reach that level. You already know from your past experiences that when you get to a certain number of dives, and you feel you are gaining skill and momentum, you wished you hadn't delayed starting the process. As you gain experience with facing your fears and creating successes you will learn that starting isn't all that bad and you may actually relish the early wobbles. The more you are wobbling, the more you are attempting to learn and accomplish. When and if other people criticize or make fun of you for wobbling, you can feel sorry for them for being imprisoned in their castle of mediocrity. Just tell them that armchair quarterbacks and hecklers are those who are too afraid to actually DO things.

Stop waiting

Stop and think about this. At the end of the day, at the end of all the talking and the stories and the reasons and the excuses…at the end of all this is that fact that you need to DO something to get what you want. You need to make a decision, make an investment of time, energy, money. You need to take a step. After all the therapy and talking and whatnot…it's just *this:* **take the next step.**

The hardest therapeutic advice I've ever been given is:

" **At the end of the day, either you will or you won't."** — Dr. Hyatt

So, there it is resting squarely on your shoulders. Your life is up to you. DO it already… DO YOUR LIFE.

~ EXERCISE ~ Make a list of any goals and dreams that you are procrastinating on. For each one include how long this has gone on.

At the end of the day, what counts the most is what you actually do and get done. You know this in your heart of hearts to be true, regardless of how you, at times, try to convince yourself otherwise.

Most of the "problems" I encounter with people usually end up at a crossroads of some combination of the following, or similar, ideas:
- They want to do something for themselves
- They want to stop doing things or stop people from doing things to them
- They want to change/be different/be "themselves"

And they can't do this because...
- They don't feel good enough
- They don't feel they "should" or don't have permission
- They are afraid of losing relationships
- They need other people to overly approve of them and their every step

We have gone over these ideas from multiple angles throughout the book in the hopes of pointing out the fact that mostly these problems are fictions and old stories designed to protect us in some way, and now they are preventing you from being and doing what you want.

DOing is where the rubber hits the road and you put your new philosophy, values and plans into action. DOing is how you become who you are. DOing is how you get what you want.

Avoiding the Work

DOing will always be superior to not-doing. Regardless of what the non-doer says about his non-doing…his words will be a platitude. It will be "imaginary points" in a game that serves other people and/or a belief system. The story and excuse will be a salve of *more pleasant feelings* that help to cover up and hide the ugly feelings and truth.

The first truth is that the non-doer wants more than he is willing to DO to get it. It may be that fear is greater than willingness. There are only two paths out of this quagmire. The first is to overcome fear and get more DOing done. The second is to lower your standards and live with less. Either or both can be appropriate at times. There is a cost to pursuing the Nth degree, and not everything in your life *needs* to reach the Nth degree. At some point we run out of time and resources and have to make compromises based on our highest values.

The Path to Personal Power

A great many people lie to themselves. They make up reasons, excuses and stories to get them out of the angst that is produced by the double bind of "I really want to, but I'm afraid to." Actually, these people would say it in the more cowardly way of "I want to but I can't." If their lies worked, then it wouldn't be so repulsive a lifestyle. The problem is, no matter how hard you try to convince yourself, you *know* inside that you are letting yourself off the hook. As Thoreau said famously, "The mass of men lead lives of quiet desperation."

To lighten the load of self-deception, desperation and regret, non-doers often prefer to hang out with other non-doers. They do *not* like to hang out with people who are having and doing what they themselves really want. These people act as mirrors—reminders of what they *could* be having and doing but are too afraid to do.

Where do non-doers flock together? Clubs and groups that demand agreement to their belief systems and rules. They want you to agree and to follow. They profit from your belief/following. They want sheeple. The non-doers get nothing in return—no real learning, no real gains. Non-doers follow the rules to collect imaginary points for their "correct" behaviors. They also get to feel morally superior for their lack of doing. I personally prefer to rebel against the made-up rules and forgo the imaginary points. DOing produces real results, unlike following belief systems which produces nothing.

Occult, new-age and other alt-spiritual groups are another place to find non-doers reveling in their belief systems. Doing rituals in your mom's basement to improve your power, financial status and sexual attractiveness is a great way to puff up your ego and achieve nothing besides running down the clock of your life. The original occult groups hid themselves for a reason…mostly because their thinking was too progressive for the current authority structures in power. They dared to elevate themselves and demanded their own experiences of what lies beyond instead of taking others' words for it. They were willing to seek and tell the truth. Unfortunately, the current iteration of these groups are seldom interested in doing real work to improve themselves and overcome fears.

Non-doers also like to spend many years in therapies of different kinds. They like to dwell in their story and make connections with others who like to do the same. I've often thought of creating some psychological trauma playing cards. This way people could easily lay them out on the table to compare and contrast with others' cards. Driving down the road of life looking in the rearview mirror is painful and is not a good strategy for making real progress.

Victims of various hardships—real and imagined (politics and most social issues)—also flock together. Numerous groups feel "owed" by the world for its lack of fairness. Their doctrines seldom include the hard work that *they* need to do, yet a lot of things that *other people* need to do to make things right. Victimhood is the common factor among many groups of non-doers. They may be victims of the past, themselves, other people, evil forces…the list is almost endless. Keep in mind that victims and true believers are very easy to control.

> **Each time you make a decision about whether to DO something, ask yourself if you want to serve your fears and the past or serve your true potential.**

At the end of the day, it mostly comes down to fear. Fear of being weak, incompetent, not-knowing, looking silly, screwing up, embarrassing yourself, smelling bad, bleeding on the rug, vomiting, shitting your pants. Fear of altering relationships and not being liked unconditionally all of the time. All of these fears feel just a little too close to the feeling of NOT GOOD ENOUGH and the "idea" of not being worthwhile deep down inside.

When you avoid *doing,* your fidelity is to the past, to the story, to your fears and to your neurology as it has been shaped thus far in life. Is your fidelity to all of *that* greater than your fidelity to your *potential*? Answer that through your actions, not through words. The following is a great question to write down and remember when you hesitate to DO things:

> *Do I want more of my past, and what I'm currently experiencing, or do I want the rewards of fulfilling my potential?*

> **Are your past limitations, hurts and disappointments really worth bringing forward in your life anymore?**

Doing is KING.

Masturbation is not sex.
Reading blogs is not lifting weights.
Watching *YouTube* is not skydiving.
You can't fake juggling or unicycling.
Daydreaming does not add to your bank balance.

Being a Legend in Your Own Mind helps nobody.

This entire book supports your "why." How you got here, where you came from, how a lot of your crap is not your fault and how some of the "games" work. It may not be your fault, it may have hurt a lot, and it may be difficult. The entire book also supports your "what"—the self and life you want to create.

Get on with your "What."

Get on with your DOing.

Get Busy.

Chinese Proverb
The best time to plant a tree was 20 years ago.
The second best time is *NOW*.

Find out if you have "external forces" thwarting you at every turn, or if your limitations are only contained in internal thought/emotion loops. ***Find out*** if your worst fears will come true. ***Find out*** if there are still monsters under your bed.

Tempt the fates!

Become who you are, there are no guarantees.

Chapter 23
Get Busy—Tips & Tricks for Success

In this chapter I share some of my favorite ideas that you can put into action to help you to add momentum and/or to get you unstuck. Many of these points have much more depth than what I've presented.

Make Haste Slowly—This was one of Dr. Hyatt's favorite maxims. Despite his high standards and demands, he was quick to point out how trying too hard and doing too much was detrimental to progress. *To grow and develop* your mind and body need to rest and process what they have taken in. Progress is enhanced by this, not slowed. When you do too much on top of what you have just done, you are not only wasting time, but may reverse the progress you have made! Slow and steady often wins the race, while impatience often spoils it. Exercise, hypnosis, Radical Undoing, therapy and limiting your sleep are all examples. If you do not heed this self-enhancing warning, you may be in danger of *killing the golden goose*—which means no more golden eggs for you.

Repetition is the Mother of Learning—Malcom Gladwell posits in his book *Outliers* that it takes around 10,000 hours to achieve mastery in many pursuits. If that is the case, the sooner you start practicing the better. Keep in mind that while some things in life are happenstantial or determined by genetics, much success in life is helped along substantially by hard work.

Do One Thing Different—Besides being the title of a great book by Bill O'Hanlon, it is a simple, solution-oriented approach to life and a great starting point when you are stuck.

Learn to Think in Contexts and Probabilities—This comes from the late Robert Anton Wilson. Also useful is Annie Duke's book, *Thinking in Bets*. Look at each decision you make in terms of the prob-

The Path to Personal Power

ability of success. In each context, your odds may change. Thinking like this helps focus you on the *what and how* of what needs to be done. It helps you to hone your critical thinking as it pushes you to measure as many variables as you can. For example, if you want to open a restaurant, you need to know the demographics of your client base and traffic patterns to get an idea of how many and what type of people could come in. Having a dream to open a Cambodian vegetarian restaurant in a small southern town on a back road is a flop waiting to happen, regardless of how passionate you are. This same idea in a hip part of Manhattan could be a huge success.

Thinking in contexts and probabilities helps you to not take things personally. Not everything works all the time for everyone everywhere. If your vegetarian restaurant doesn't work out, it may not mean you are a bad chef. When you don't take it personally, you will be up for taking more calculated risks. Many successful people have failed multiple times and kept on going.

Get in Front of Your Inspiration—Inspiration is like gasoline on a fire. You are responsible for refilling your tank. What is inspires you? What do you need to do to be around what inspires you? I like to watch movies and documentaries about interesting and successful people. Reading, hiking, going to a museum, art fair or vintage car show are further examples. It is up to you to seek out and cultivate your inspiration.

Dust Off Your Curiosity—What are you interested in? What would you like to play with? What would you like to find out more about? What would you like to try? Curiosity is the antidote to boredom and often can jumpstart you out of being stuck.

Just Show Up—So much in life comes from just showing up. Be on time, be prepared to offer an opinion and to work hard. Few people are. I can't stress how many opportunities are missed because of not showing up. People don't care about your excuses. They care about how you can add value to them and what they are doing. It is easy to win a race when nobody else shows up.

Kaizen (improvement)—*One Small Step Can Change Your Life: The Kaizen Way* by Robert Maurer discusses how shooting for a 1% improvement can cause great things to change down the line.

Directions Instead of Goals—Sometimes it is more useful to set a direction instead of a specific goal. While goals can be motivating, they aren't the end-all for all people in all contexts. Deciding to lose 20 pounds is a goal, while becoming healthier is a direction. Healthier can encompass eating, exercise, stretching and drinking more water in addition to your weight on the scale. What you accomplish heading in this direction might be better and broader than one specific goal.

Focus on Behaviors—Whether you are setting a goal or a direction, your focus should be on engaging in specific actions, not on the end result. Losing 20 pounds or becoming healthier are end results. The actions that you take every day are the means to get there. Your leverage is at the decision point of your *behaviors,* not at the decision point when the goal or direction is set. Many people make the *resolution* and think that this is the important step. The important steps are the little ones. Each small behavior is the decision point that determines success or failure.

Your Reminder Story—I have found it very helpful to keep "why" I'm pursuing what I am pursuing front-of-mind. Much of the content of this book I keep readily at hand to remind myself of the what's, why's and why not's of where I want to go. Dr. Hyatt used to say that if he woke me up in the middle of the night, I should know what I was about and where I was headed.

Give Yourself What You Need—A Ferrari is a high performance car, and it is optimized for performance. Because of this, it needs more maintenance and more tuning. It is sensitive to proper adjustments. You shouldn't expect it to behave like a Honda, which is maximized for dependability and ease of maintenance. As you are maximizing your life, you will probably find that you make better progress if you give yourself what you need instead what you *would like to not have to need.* You may need more sleep or need to be around people who are nice to you (and not ones that hassle you). You may find yourself becoming more sensitive, which is a good thing. I once bought some high-quality stainless silverware. Inside the packaging it explained that the product was made of *stainless* steel and not *stain-free* steel. While it is hard and durable, it is not indestructible. It will scratch and wear over time, and if handled without care it can be damaged beyond repair. You will make better and more comfortable progress in the work if you are real instead of trying to be ultra-hard and stain-free. A corollary to this is making sure you **Don't Kill the Golden Goose.** Working hard, burning the midnight oil and stretching your comfort zone are all skills of mastery. When these tools become a lifestyle, your risk burnout and injury. You may also burn out or injure others. As the story goes, greed makes you work the goose a little harder, a little longer, until one day it is burned out and pissed off and stops laying golden eggs completely. You are the goose. Take care of yourself and those who partner with you.

Follow the Instructions—Whether following a workout plan, cooking a meal or mixing a craft cocktail, there are often instructions written by experienced masters. These clear, laid-out paths to success offer you a shortcut to learning and mastery. If you follow the instructions, if you use the techniques and ingredients and measurements, you will quickly be able to produce a wonderful outcome. Some people have fragile egos that, unless allowed free reign to improvise at whim, feel "uninspired" and "restricted" when following directions. They tend to "wing it" and "improvise." The problem with improvising is that if you do so before you know the basics, you will produce *crap*. "Improvisation" on a musical instrument that you can't really play is a polite way of saying that you are making noise pollution. In exercise it can get you seriously injured, and with cooking and cocktails you get inedible experiments and wasted ingredients. When doing the *work,* you will get random results—*at best*—if you don't follow the instructions. If you enjoy psychological suffering, ignore this paragraph. Just don't call me looking for sympathy. If you heed this paragraph and begin to approach mastery, others may enjoy experiencing your riffs and you may make a name for yourself.

Set Priorities—You can't do and learn everything all at once. If everything is important, nothing is.

Do Something Self-Enhancing That Makes You Uncomfortable—Develop a thicker skin by stretching yourself. Not only do you increase skill and make progress, you also make it easier to make faster progress by getting more used to being uncomfortable.

> **Measure and value what you *do*, not what you say.**

Relating

Chapter 24
Playing Well With Others

The topic of *healthy* relationships is not discussed often enough. People are treated as objects to get something *from* or to do something *to*. In my professional experience, relationships are common hang-ups and sources of angst for most people.

The ability to start and manage relationships is an important area to understand and master. There are three primary reasons for this. The first and most obvious reason is that other humans can be a great source of pleasure, joy and entertainment. The second and equally obvious reason is the simple fact that much of your success in life is directly tied to your ability to work well with others. This includes working towards common goals, providing and exchanging value with others and getting things done through/with others. The third and less obvious reason is that *healthy and powerful relationships* are the sole domain of those with true power, because to have that rare type of relationship, you must overcome both yourself and yourself in *relation* to others.

You are formed through relationships. You develop rules and expectations about people that you then project onto others. You form rules and generalizations about how the world works and then expect to see those maintained. The failure to explore and reset these notions usually leads to suffering and dysfunction both in the individual and in relationships—to both other people and the world at large.

You are free to have whatever types of relationships you like with others, including not having relationships. Free in terms of choice and preference, as well as freedom from socially standardized notions of "right" and "wrong. Homosexuality, bisexuality, being alone and being childless (or, as some say, child-free) are examples of preferences and decisions that can be viewed through the lens of being self-enhancing, regardless of the beliefs and expectations of others.

Your freedom to choose does not guarantee that others will play along with you and your ideas. Just as it's not your primary purpose or focus to *be and give* everything that others demand from you—remember, this is also not the primary focus of others in relationship with you. This is an important point, because, in my professional experience, many adults never seem to grow out of the self-centric world view of a young child—at least not enough.

Whether we are talking about romantic relationships, friendships, work relationships, neighbors or co-inhabitants of this planet—it is worth looking into your biases, preconceptions, needs and patterned responses and resetting these as necessary. This is more functional than leaving them set on "repeat history" mode, which is usually the button pressed during our development.

What happens when we don't reset our expectations from "repeat history" mode? Your best results and most accurate predictions about outcomes with other people occur when those around you are most similar to those around you at the time of imprint. This is because you calculate probable outcomes based on a very small number of experiences with only a few people and then project these onto the entire population. What often ends up happening is that our predictions and expectations are significantly off, as not everyone responds in the way we think they "should." Your expectations are therefore skewed towards a certain outcome. For example, if your parents were very lenient and lazy, you may have a tough time with your boss who actually expects quality work done on time. On the other hand, people who were raised by hyper-critical parents often expect others in positions of authority to be like that and might have trouble asking for a promotion or raise.

People tend to repeat history and have a knack for putting themselves into new relationships that are almost identical to those in their past. They attempt to "get it right" and restore what was lost. (Hmmm... Could this also correlate with metaphysical value and the *concept* of deservingness?) This is analogous to a mouse looking for cheese in a new maze in the same place it was in the old maze.

Consider your stance in the world. Reflect on how you present yourself, how tall you stand, how confidently you walk, the valence through which you look at yourself to assess your self-worth and value. What you expect to be "allowed" to get out of life may be significantly different than what others are willing to give. They may, in fact, be willing to give you *more* than you are expecting!

At times you will rate yourself more highly than others do. This results in your not meeting expectations and perhaps getting less favorable outcomes than you had planned. Other times you will rate yourself lower than others do, resulting in more favorable outcomes than you were expecting.

There is an important caveat here: very few people do the necessary work ***because of their beliefs.*** How many people put in a good effort when they are expecting rejection? Almost none. This creates a self-fulfilling prophecy and strengthens the original belief (map). Robert Anton Wilson famously said that *"Reality is what you can get away with."* This means that if you are open to it and willing to wholeheartedly test reality, *it may indeed be more favorably disposed to you than you originally **thought** it was!* You will only find out if you test it, and testing makes most people uncomfortable. If you never test it, you will never know and will never reach your potential.

When the process of testing the map against reality is applied to other people, several good things become available to you. First, you open the opportunity of getting an instant level upgrade and internal promotion—you aren't so bad after all—you are better than you thought you were. Second, you take others off the hook for having to rate you a certain way. You stop squeezing them for validation or blaming them for being so hard on you. Third, if you have been over-rating yourself, then you learn that you need to put a little more effort into your relationships and work—and that **it's not personal.** It's not about *you per se,* it's just that your level of effort needs to increase if you want your results in reality to match the high level you've been rating yourself.

Resetting this map is a part of your individual work. It is also a part of how you evaluate others and your world. Your self-ideas need to be re-evaluated and reset, and your ideas about other people and the world at large also need to be reset…if you want to be more successful in your relationships and in life in general. If you are rigorous in this, you will find that your odds of success and happiness in life, especially in those areas that involve other people, are greatly increased.

Chapter 25
Relationships & Development

We all enter this world completely **dependent** on others for all of our survival and developmental needs. As we age, we gradually begin to gain control of ourselves and our world. As previously mentioned, humans have a long developmental period. Infants have absolute physical dependence for survival for several years. As children develop, socialization and formal education are added to the mix. To be successful, these require additional levels of physical and psychological support, along with other resources. As we grow, we begin to become more self-reliant and **independent.** In our society, we might say that full independence is reached at the age of 18, after compulsory education is complete and we are granted status as legal adults.

There are many ways this process can go awry. Often these hiccups are overcome and chalked up to learning. Some of these issues are extreme enough, consistent enough or happen at a sensitive time where they become *maladaptations.*

The role of others in our personal development plays an enormous part in how we view ourselves, others and the world at large. It is often said that nobody has a "normal" childhood, and despite parents' best efforts, no one comes out unscathed. Our protracted childhood and slow cognitive and emotional development (as a species) is often as much to blame as outright traumas and abuse. You might refer back to Chapter 14 (Imaginary Problems & Limitations) and Chapter 15 (Picking Up the Pieces).

We develop under the watchful eyes of many people. Parents, family, teachers, neighbors, politicians and police all participate. We develop in contexts that we did not choose: race, religion, nationality, spiritual orientation, political orientation, parents, family, socioeconomic status. Many of our beliefs, preferences and rules about life are adopted at an early age before critical thinking is available.

Think about our inherent survival instincts and the implications around the importance of staying within our "tribe." For most of human history, being kicked out of one's tribe meant almost certain death. Few are able to provide food and shelter for themselves in a hostile environment (other tribes, animals, weather). Our ability to "fit in and get along" first addresses our need for survival and then our developmental and psychological needs. When survival needs are threatened, and much more importantly, when they *are perceived to be threatened,* we are placed into a situation where we "have to" be out of integrity with ourselves to maintain inclusion in the tribe. What is asked of us as children sometimes runs contrary to our psychological needs and healthy development as we attempt to move from dependence to independence. Often the process of becoming an independent individual is thwarted by others, frequently unknowingly and without malicious intent. The less developed and aware the parents, and the more baggage and unresolved issues of their own, the more this happens.

As children we see ourselves through the actions and reactions of others, and we attempt to modify our behavior to get more of what we want and less of what we don't want. We adapt ourselves as best we can to the rules, values and belief systems of the adults and authorities so we can learn and get what we *think* we need in an expedient way. We watch those around us and imitate them to learn skills and to garner attention and affection. This is completely normal.

The developmental learnings that become issues needing to be re-evaluated (healed) are the ones in which the lesson/meaning/fact-of-life are *inaccurate, self-limiting and/or self-diminishing.* When these original learnings are generalized onto other people and into different contexts, they produce less than optimal results and thus cause suffering and wasted resources. I find that these learnings are often unfair to the child and are geared towards serving the authority more than assisting the child and the learning process.

Let's look at a couple of examples. A young girl is taught that a woman's place is to be subservient to her husband. She is to perform household tasks as she is told, or she is yelled at and belittled. The young girl experiences this through her parents' interactions, as well as those tasks assigned to her by her father. Both she and her mother are punished for infractions. What beliefs do you think she will adopt about herself, her role in the world as a woman, as a wife, and about men? She may become soft spoken and shy and hesitate to communicate her preferences. She may feel that she doesn't deserve an equal opinion and will often go without or do with less. She may make pleasing her father a much higher value than pleasing herself and others when making decisions. This could impact her chosen career and education, as well as where she decides to live. Her programming around relationships will likely dictate how she deals with other people in her life, from fellow students, potential mates, coworkers and authority in the workplace. In the adult world she will often use behaviors that kept her safe and in good graces *as a child*. This is less effective than many of the other attitudinal and behavioral choices available to her, yet she will often perceive other choices as *risky*.

A young boy in the same household might have a very different experience. He may grow up thinking that women exist primarily to do his bidding. How he treats women, while being normal to him, would likely be highly offensive to most women. As he interacts with fellow students, girlfriends and potential mates, coworkers and women in authority, he is confused that his behaviors do not yield the results that they are "supposed to" (i.e., what his dad historically got).

The point to keep in mind is that we did not develop and form our personalities, values, rules, concepts and conclusions about ourselves and the world in a neutral vacuum. We develop in a specific context, location and point in history. We need to understand the difference between that context and all the other options that are available to us. We need to re-examine what works best for *us*, not what honors the original context, so we can become who we truly are and wish to be.

Difficult relationships create subpar self-evaluations and generalizations about the world. We create defense mechanisms to cope and to protect our ego and self-worth. Our ideas and expectations about relationships with others are also skewed. When you combine these factors and add in the fact that few people ever intentionally think about this, it is no wonder that people can have a difficult time getting along with each other.

> "The only time I'm right is when I play along"
> — Bob Mould, *Husker Du*

Chapter 26
What Is a Healthy Relationship?

To look at what healthy relationships are, we need to start from a clean slate, and not from our personal history. A healthy relationship is not necessarily what you think it is, or were told it should be, or what it looks like in animated love stories. Part of understanding healthy relationships is understanding that what you experienced firsthand growing up and what you are told to expect by most people is not necessarily what you should expect.

Dependent—We start out in this world completely dependent on others to take care of our needs. We are reliant physically for survival and emotionally for support.

As we age and develop, we gain autonomy. The process of becoming your own *self* has been called **Individuation** (notably by Carl Jung and Margaret Mahler). This is a gradual process which can last well into your adult life. If this process goes well, you becomes your authentic self, which may be something quite different than what your family or others expect. There are many developmental milestones and rites of passage that lead to healthy individuation. Properly going to the bathroom, dressing yourself, going to school on your own, choosing sports and interests, creating friendships, first jobs and romantic relationships are just a few examples. We learn to develop (hopefully) healthy boundaries and an acceptance of differences. We become conscious and responsible for our choices and decisions and gradually take on more responsibility, accountability and ownership for ourselves and our lives.

If the process of individuation goes well, we become **Independent**. We think, speak, make life choices and act for *ourselves as the primary beneficiary*. This means that you do not "need" others for physical, emotional and economic wellbeing. This is readily labeled

The Path to Personal Power 141

as "selfish" by those who need you to "need" them. A fully independent person does not need to edit themselves for others. Their interests, preferences, strengths and weaknesses are fine by them. They are good enough. They are self-actualizing and able to learn as they go. They are not defined by their past, by their story *or by other people*.

If the process of individuation goes poorly, however, we may become **Pathologically Dependent.** This means that you are dependent upon others for your own personal value. Such people are not self-defining and self-actualizing without the involvement and approval of others. They are overly sensitive to the approval of others. The desire to be *needed* is a partially developed version of being *desirable and worthy of love*. Most importantly, they do not see themselves as *worthy of being their own person*. (Yes, metaphysical value once again.) Dependent people cannot be happy and fulfilled without the support and approval of others. Sometimes these people feel and act as a conjoined part of a relationship, not as an individual person.

No one has their developmental process go perfectly smoothly, so most of us are stuck somewhere between dependency and independence. It is a most worthy challenge to complete the journey to independence to the best of our ability as a fully free individual is best equipped to maximize his creative potential. Anything less than this results in a compromise between what you can do and become—your potential—and the interests of others.

When individuals who are approaching greater levels of independence come together, they have the opportunity to develop an **Interdependent** relationship. This is a relationship between equals who do not need or depend on each other. They are self-reliant psychologically, physically and economically. They take full responsibility for their happiness and life outcomes. Because of their self-reliance, they can *choose* to support each other without playing games.

Your goal is to develop enough personal power and autonomy to become *Independent* and *Interdependent*. If your expectations have been less than this, then you know where your relationship problems stem from.

Stop Playing Games

As we develop, we learn to play games to balance the need to be an individual and to continue to get our needs met from our family or "tribe." We learn to hide differences and shortcomings when others are not accepting of them. People learn to agree, to avoid saying "no," and to forgo acting in their own best interests to get what they want.

Keep in mind that most relationships involve compromise. We are all different and have differing needs and interests. Living from a place of *absolutely no compromise* is not the solution. This is a childish fight against how the world works, and a position people often take when in conflict. Extremes are much cheaper and easier than dialogue and negotiation.

Your expectations and rules for those in relationships with you should be on the table. This means that you should communicate them overtly and directly. It also means there are no "hidden rules behind the rules" and no-strings-attached after those rules.

Relationships are not vehicles to abdicate your own personal responsibility. It is YOUR job to:

- Find your own happiness
- Create financial wellbeing
- Determine what you aim for in life
- Find motivation and support yourself in your goals
- Give yourself permission
- Set your own values and definition of success
- Decide what is **not** your job and responsibility

People who are independent and interdependent do not need to play games to get what they want in life. They have their relationship contracts on-the-table instead of under-the-table. Another way to say this is that expectations and costs are explicit and overt.

If your expectations are different from what I've written about *independence* and *interdependence,* then this is where your relationship problems are coming from.

> **As a species, we have the *opportunity* to communicate and work together to solve our collective and (at times) our individual problems.**

Chapter 27
The Solitary Path

The journey to mastery is trod on a SOLITARY PATH. To have a life that is different from the one those around you are living (and perhaps signing you up for), you will need to, in some ways, leave others behind.

Your friends and family cannot all go with you to college. Not everyone wants to go to the ballet or rodeo with you. Not everyone wants to go to the planetarium or the ball game.

Even when others share your interests and passions, they may not share them to the same degree. Your friends and fellow math students may not want to get their Ph.D. in math. The friends you meet taking guitar lessons may not want to be in a band or make a band their career.

Where things get tricky is in relationships where others feel threatened in some way by your interests, differences, skills and success. Most mammals view differences as risky, at least at first glance. Egos are easily bruised and status, real or imagined, is easily threatened.

Consider the first child in a family to go to college. Some parents tell their kids from an early age that they are going to college, no matter what, so they can have better opportunities in life. The college student is exposed to new subjects and areas of study. Eventually they will demonstrate their knowledge in the presence of their parents and some will hear a comment such as, "So, you think you are better than us now?" or "You think you are smarter than me?" The child is now in a double bind. Either he wanted to go on his own accord with the understanding that education betters his prospects, and/or his parents understood this as well. But in either case the parents now feel threatened, and because of that they defend themselves with the threat of exclusion or removal of support and love.

College is an example of pushback that happens later in life. The parents who respond to their own emotions and insecurities in the above example do this much earlier as well. Examples:

- Do you really need that many crayons for school? We only had pencils and chalk.
- I didn't own a bicycle until I was 18.
- Not everybody in the world has a birthday party every year.
- Do you really want to stay overnight at your friend's house and upset your mother?
- I didn't have a car/phone/toy/experience when I was a kid…

By the time many big decisions arise in life, there is a precedent of conflict around choosing for yourself caused by an ingrained pattern of "I want to but I can't." Decisions that enhance yourself will be obvious logically yet accompanied by shame, guilt and/or anxiety. Instead of its being easy and natural to act in accordance with your best interests, there is now friction, *perhaps to the point of having to choose between preserving a relationship or maximizing your own potential.*

Because the feelings of abandonment and withdrawal of love are so powerful and connected to your self-worth, they create the double-bind of deciding whether to stay in the tribe and survive or go off on your own to survive. It's not necessary that the threat of abandonment, withdrawal of love and support *be real*—the *fear* of it is often enough to force a decision. Thus, it is not uncommon that children make decisions based on *other people's* whims, emotions and best interests instead of their own. This does not necessarily change in adulthood or perhaps in their entire life.

In the previous example where the parents are threatened by their child's new knowledge, the "correct" response or perspective is most likely not something the child has come across:

Parents: "You think you are smarter than me now? You think you are better than me?"

Child: "Well, that was the whole fucking point all along, wasn't it?! You insist I go to school, now you are all bent up over your own idea…because it worked? You should be high-fiving me right now because I'm telling you about physics and history!"

The Path to Personal Power

This example is not fictional, but rather one I have experienced in my professional work with clients. The next example is personal to me, and just too good not to share with you.

Relative: "You are wearing a polo shirt, with a collar on it. That's pretty fancy. You must think you are better than me."

Me: "What I'm wearing is basically a t-shirt with a collar sewn on it. Are you fucking insane? You're kidding, right?"

Heaven forbid that you get an education, wear something nice, eat a fabulous dinner, order a nice glass of red wine, take a vacation, get in shape, meet interesting people or accomplish more than the bare minimum. In fact, these things may be necessary to be in certain company or necessary to achieve your ends!

The Path reveals its solitary nature at these junctions, even if just for the duration of the argument. Your decisions are your own, and the reactions of others are their own. It is important that you consider and prepare for the negative reactions of others so that you can make decisions in your own best interests and not be deterred by the oft-recurring poor behavior and insecurity of others.

The decision to pursue the path of self-mastery is the first and primary point of the path. It is a decision that you must make alone—no one that can make the decision for you or with you. If you need others to convince you that everything will be alright, or to hold your hand along the way, then you have not yet decided that you alone will do what it takes. Think about the times you committed to a course of action. In the split second this takes, it happens *inside* yourself—it is an inner revelation and an inner momentum. If you do not have this inner sensation, you haven't really decided. If you have this inner sensation and choose not to follow it then you are out of integrity with yourself.

A second and equally important point is that if you are serious about pursuing the path of self-mastery you will have to be strong enough in yourself to allow others to leave the path at their own exit. It is not that you *need to* leave others behind, but you will certainly find that others will not commit to themselves as much as you will.

This doesn't mean that you must leave your family or can't spend time with friends. You don't need to make a formal declaration that you are special. It simply means that you cannot and should not expect others to join you or understand your priorities. You cannot coerce others into joining you, and if for some reason you do convince them, you will have done it on *your* power, and then your progress (and most likely the lack of it) is tied to theirs.

We are sold a bill of goods about how human relationships and interactions *should be*. Ideals are reinforced by television, society and our own personal needs (of course the *feelings* make these *real* and thus *enforceable,* both upon you and others).

The following story comes to mind:

> One night I had a dream—
> I dreamed I was walking along the beach with the Lord and across the sky flashed scenes from my life.
> For each scene I noticed two sets of footprints,
> one belonged to me and the other to the Lord.
> When the last scene of my life flashed before me,
> I looked back at the footprints in the sand.
> I noticed that many times along the path of my life,
> there was only one set of footprints.
> I also noticed that it happened at the very lowest
> and saddest times in my life.
> This really bothered me and I questioned the Lord about it.
> "Lord, you said that once I decided to follow you,
> you would walk with me all the way,
> but I have noticed that during the most troublesome times in my life
> there is only one set of footprints.
> I don't understand why in times when I needed you most, you should leave me."
> The Lord replied, "My precious, precious child,
> I love you and I would never, never leave you
> during your times of trial and suffering.
> When you saw only one set of footprints,
> it was then that I carried you."
>
> — Mary Stevenson, *Footprints in the Sand*

The Path to Personal Power

The first time I read this I wept inconsolably. I was probably 12 years old at the time. How I wanted to believe I was carried during the times I suffered! How sweet this was to have faith and get this in return! I learned the truth of the matter much later in life: when the going got tough, the footprints I saw were *mine*. I had picked myself up and kept on going. Whether or not there are other people involved, how you respond to life is *your* decision.

Certainly, it is a great blessing to have those who love and care about you by your side during life's difficulties. It is a greater blessing and gift to yourself to love and support yourself enough—to believe in yourself enough—to keep going. If you need to always see two or more sets of footprints in the sand, then personal power and progress, especially along this path, is probably not going to happen. Remember that no matter how much other people help and prop you up, it is still *your* feet underneath you and your decision to stand on them.

> Nobody can carry you on this path. At least not very far.

Another implication of the solitary path is that nobody can do your work for you. Even the language of *helping you* is inaccurate. Another person may be able to point out certain things, but you need to do the work and find *your* way yourself.

If others volunteer to *overly* help you, politely decline. They have a hidden agenda. Your work is your work, and their work is theirs.

If others ask you to help them be accountable for acting in their own best interests, politely decline. Do not ask others to help you be accountable or remind you to be the best you can be. It's up to you to do this for yourself. Your journey in life is not a joint responsibility.

Just as nobody can do the work for you, you cannot do the work for them. You cannot make them do it, and if you force it on them or carry them, you will eventually be sorry. When you carry someone or attempt to do their work for them, as soon as you put them down, they are going to kick you and beat you for "letting them down."

Life is not a three-legged race. People are not strapped to you. You may find as you progress in your work that people change and that you need to update your rules, boundaries and expectations. Your changes may not be easy for them to adapt to, and you should expect this in advance.

The erroneous belief that you cannot "do it" on your own is exactly what will keep you sitting on the sidelines of life, waiting for permission, waiting for a guarantee that others will unconditionally love and accept you, or waiting for other people to come along on the ride to support you. The more waiting, the more you forget your own power and resiliency. The more this withers away, the harder it is to get it back.

Don't take this to mean that you shouldn't be nice to others and helpful to them. It also doesn't mean that you should tolerate people actively discouraging you or bringing you down.

Loneliness is not the same as the *alone-ness* that I speak of. The point of decision and real commitment is something that happens personally and within yourself. It happens *alone,* within yourself, regardless of who is around and who/where the data came from. Think deeply about this as you recall your own moments of decision and commitment.

Chapter 28
Elitism & Being Liked

As you work on this path with diligence and persistence you will begin to get good results. It seems that personal power, with its aspects of awareness, skill and self-calibration, is much like a flywheel. It takes a lot of energy to get it going, yet once it gets going it isn't hard to maintain its momentum and potential power. The incremental gains and the subsequent successes that you have seem to come easier and more often. Fortune favors the bold and those who work hard.

This is a wonderful discovery…for *you*. Yet you may find that others don't share your joy and enthusiasm around your success and personal gains.

As you work hard, you move further out on the bell curve. Statistically speaking, you find that the higher you progress, the fewer people there are at your level of achievement. For example, the current world record for the deadlift is 1,102 pounds (as of 2018). There are only a handful of people in the world who can lift 1,000 pounds, but quite a few who can lift 500. The amount of time, dedication, persistence and suffering required to go from 500 to 1,000 to 1,100 is what culls the many from the few in this endeavor. The work you are putting into yourself on this path is similar.

Your goal may not be to become "better" than others, and if you are psychologically developed, you probably won't consider yourself better than others in an ***absolute*** way, just different and more effective in some areas. Nevertheless, you will be looked at as being better, and not everyone is going to be supportive of this.

If you can lift 500 pounds, you can say that this is "better" in a *relative* way than lifting 350. You can do more work. If you have a million dollars in the bank, you could also say that this is better than having $27.50. You have more spending ability. If your body fat percentage is 15%, we can also say this is better than 35% as it is better looking and statistically healthier. The list goes on and on, and if you refer back to the stereo equalizer analogy in Chapter 20 (What Do You Want?) you will remember that one aim is to be working on raising the bar on each area of life that is important to you, along with some—like physical health—that are universally self-enhancing.

I often hear a lot of whining and disagreement when I say that some things are better than others. This is because the average person doesn't (more likely cannot) separate the idea of relative *better* from that of absolute *better* (metaphysical value). So, any claim of *better* makes them feel lesser, anxious and threatened. Heated arguments often follow:

- Money isn't the only measure of happiness or success.
- You can't take it with you.
- That guy is going to have problems with his back when he's older.
- You can't say that a Ferrari is necessarily better than a Ford. They both take you from point A to point B.
- You don't need a Swiss watch to tell the time, you can just use your phone.

While these may have some truth in them, I call bullshit. People are downright afraid to admit that in most cases a Ferrari is a better piece of machinery than the Kia sedan they are sitting in. People already know they are overweight and feel bad about it, but instead of getting busy they talk about genetics and luck and excuses. So when you find yourself getting ***"better"*** and having success…here comes the punchline:

Do not expect to be liked.

Often you will be admired and congratulated for your achievements, but there is no guarantee that everyone will respond this way. There is no guarantee that your family, friends and others close to you will respond positively either. Don't expect fanfare and a round of applause. Don't expect admiration and a pat on the back, although you may get these from time to time.

You can also expect that, in some cases, you will feel uncomfortable in the spotlight as people break off eye contact, sigh, roll their eyes or whisper behind your back. Some may flat out walk away. You are

The Path to Personal Power

a mirror to other people and, when they don't like what they see, don't be surprised if they get peeved at the mirror—you. Other people are engaging in "despair math"[1] all the time—measuring and comparing themselves to you. It is not your fault that they have despair in their shortcomings. In fact, your *being better* may be a gift to them. If you find yourself questioning if it's your fault that others feel bad, consider a different question: "Do they despair *enough* to get motivated?"

The path to mastery does not exclude others, nor does it insist that they come along. In terms of the work, not everyone will commit to themselves and their own self-enhancement as much as you will. This is a fact that you should recognize and prepare for. Not everyone will agree that they are best served by engaging in more self-enhancing behaviors than self-diminishing ones. This is not your concern or responsibility. It is theirs.

The approval of others is neither a good motivation nor validation. In fact, the disapproval of the herd is often a great measure that you are succeeding in creating yourself and your life into a work of art! If you aren't ruffling some feathers here and there, then you aren't trying hard enough.

As you find yourself achieving your ends, you can be graceful, offer to assist and show a little humility around others. Whatever you do…

> **Don't apologize.**

Do not apologize for winning. Do not apologize that you worked long and hard to reach your goals. Do not apologize for the luxuries and opportunities that befall you because of this. Why? Apologies put yourself down a notch in an attempt to keep rapport with someone else. Do not be *sorry* that you are working to make yourself and your life a self-styled work of art.

I suggest that the best approach in these situations is to remind others that it is great to win and remind them that they too can do it if they are willing to work for it. This comes up often for me because I

---

[1] For more on Despair Math and a test you can take yourself, see the chapter "Danger: Thinking Causes Brain Growth" in Christopher S. Hyatt's *The Psychopath's Bible,* Falcon Press.

do this for a living. Once in a while you may serve as an inspiration to others.

How tall you stand and your ability to persist in the light of not being liked *because* of your efforts is a great measure of your personal power and your commitment to yourself.

At times other people may go further with their disdain than you would like. Mostly they will be silent as you tell your tales, as they secretly begin to panic that you might actually succeed. At times they will discourage you. Some will leave you. The threat of the withdrawal of love, abandonment or violence are the same tactics that are used upon children to create an aversion to "standing out." Those buttons are still effective on most people.

I suggest that you proceed thoughtfully when this happens and think deeply on whether you really want people like this around you. Examine your own need to be liked. By how many people? All of the time? Under what circumstances is this useful? Learn to pick yourself up because you love and cherish yourself. Don't expect to be liked all the time by everyone. In fact, have you ever challenged the belief that you are "supposed to" be liked by everyone all the time? This may be a belief that is hiding somewhere in your mind like a stowaway you didn't know was onboard.

It is called "the road less traveled" for a good reason. Most sheeple quit and fall short of their potential in order to remain in the good graces of the herd. Don't let that be your reason to quit.

~ EXERCISE ~

Ponder the following:

Will the fear of standing alone be the reason you give up?

If you give up on yourself and whore yourself out for the praise and approval of others, will the arrival of that praise and approval make you a virgin again?

Waking Up

Chapter 29
What's Wrong With Just *Being*?

I guess it is fair to call this section of the book the part about "spiritual" development. The philosophy presented up to this point in this book sets you up well to pursue this part of the work. Unlike most systems of self-development, instead of being threatened by the idea of waking up, this one points you toward it. The philosophy presented up to now in this book is analogous to having a ladder. It helps you to climb, to have a higher perspective and to elevate yourself. When you reach the top of the ladder and step onto that next level, you no longer need the ladder. It was a necessary part of your climb, and has served you well, even if you are no longer standing on it. It is an outstanding ladder in that *it works*.

If you are interested only in reaching the top of the ladder and staying at the higher rungs, that's your business. There is no right or wrong about it. Just do your fellow travelers a courtesy and don't speak about things on the next level that you don't know, haven't experienced for yourself, or are afraid to explore. (I read a blog recently where the author insisted that meditation accomplished nothing and was a waste of time...because he had tried it ***once.***)

Though the analogy of a ladder is useful, it is also misleading in that it implies a destination—the top of the ladder. Success has many metaphors, such as higher, farther, *more,* faster, etc. While material success may fit into these, for the most part your true self does not because it is before and beyond these ideas.

The concept of a *destination* is a powerful and brilliant illusion. It is the solving of problems. As a metaphor it works up to a certain point. More stuff, less suffering, but it never fulfills its promise to you, which is personal completion, wholeness, fulfillment and peace.

The destination is a part of the promise of *more,* where we started this adventure together in Chapter 1 (The Call of *More*)...where I said that the subpar life isn't worth living. At some point on your journey, as you succeed in making yourself and your life into a work of art, you may find that this is still not enough. This might be because even though you have maximized your *self,* you are still stuck with the limitations of a *self.* Waking up is about transcending that *self* and its shackles. It is fully knowing what you are. It is about transcending the fear and illusion that comes with a disconnected self.

There are many schools of thought that have you start with and only focus on waking up. There are also many paths that only discuss the pursuit of *more* and of personal power. There is no right, wrong or necessarily better, although it is my experience that working on waking up is easier from a confident and relaxed place—one that has more luxuries of free time, space and resources. It is harder to tell someone who is suffering that neither his problems nor his self is real. Working on the pursuit of *more* and personal power provides the resources needed.

Some will tell you that suffering itself is the best impetus for change. My impetus was the suffering of feeling incomplete and of not-knowing. This came to the front more as I took care of my basic needs in life: education, career and finances. It makes sense that, without suffering, the motivation to wake up and/or the desire to change may not be there—that it may never cross your mind—and by looking around at the herd I often see this to be the case. If you can't feel the pebble in your shoe, you probably aren't motivated to look in it.

Both sides of the work—creating yourself and your life into a work of art *and* waking up—take time. So, why not do both simultaneously? What else is there to do? Why not take full advantage of the opportunity of being alive? Both sides are self-enhancing, but in different ways for different selves. As I suggested in the Introduction, you should work on the first five sections and this one in parallel.

To say there is a spiritual side to the path implies other sides. At this point, it is more accurate to say that there are no "sides" of the path at all. There is no manufactured, dualistic "fight" about good/bad, light/dark, spiritual/materialistic. These dichotomies are not necessary and serve as both a distraction and a limitation.

The Path to Personal Power

Waking up need not and should not be done in a vacuum. *Life itself* is the context in which this work is done. What other context is there? What you are attached to, cling to, run from, embrace and ignore are all done in your *regular life,* so why create a subset of life? Having grown up going to church now and again, it never made sense to me why church on Sunday was different than every other place on every other day. It is duplicitous. You are looking to apply all of this work in all contexts.

Waking up is about directly experiencing your true nature and your world *as it is*. It is about coming to know what you truly are. It is about transcending the ego and identity beyond the separate "self." It is about the direct experience of reality before the mind weighs in. Reality doesn't need the valence of mind and thought with all the labels, explanations, concepts and beliefs it insists upon.

Waking up and moving past the mind is not about acquiring something more, or adding something to yourself, or fixing what is bad, evil or broken. It is about dropping. It is about transcending mind and its byproducts. It is about removing the valence—removing the opaque, discolored lens and seeing clearly.

Waking up is about remembering something that you have forgotten to pay attention to. It is forgotten by being distracted and focused somewhere else for a long time. Have you ever searched for your keys to find them clutched in your own hand? What you are looking for hides in plain sight.

For most people, the shift to *being* is a gradual affair, so the direct experiences, the understanding and the work progress continues until you are ready and able to remain at that next level. Eventually, if you persist, there will come a time when you will have one foot on the ladder and the other foot on the next level. You may find that this step off the ladder is the same ground as the step *onto* the ladder, and that the ladder wasn't needed all that much in the first place, but *you will need the direct experience of that yourself.*

> The journey and the destination end up not being one of distance but one of *depth.*

Chapter 30
DIY Enlightenment

Over the past few years a lot of information has become available around the concept and techniques of meditation for awakening/ enlightenment. Previous to this, people have struggled looking for methods and results that they can translate into Western practice. It was hard to determine what was working...or if it was working at all. It was difficult to trust time-intensive methods without being able to gauge progress. Those who achieved results had a tough time discerning and explaining what exactly led to their changes. This caused many practitioners great frustration and many have given up. The return on investment just wasn't there.

With the advent of the internet, a lot of information has surfaced that was historically difficult to access. Difficult because much of it comes from different cultures and the translations are cumbersome. Difficult because of religious differences and non-Western values. Difficult because of misinformation and dogma.

Now people can come together and share their stories, methods and results. It is relatively easy to find people who are further along to ask questions of and to get instruction from without having to travel the globe. Different teachers, their beliefs and techniques can be explored from your home, making it easier to separate belief systems (religions) from techniques that produce real results. There is also more scientific and neurological research that supports and validates what happens to your neurology as a result of practice.

The net result of this is a renewed interest and hope of result. At a minimum, people are able to get their arrows onto the target a lot quicker. The increased information flow also allows people to verify the claims and methods of others to some extent. Instead of believing some guru hook, line and sinker and wasting lots of time and energy, people can share their experience and hone the methods to make them more expedient. Getting a map from one person is not the same as getting a map that is verified by 25 people.

Direct Experience

The DIY (Do-It-Yourself) approach to waking up is the *only* approach. It makes sense when you think about it: who else is going to do this inner work for you? The DIY aspect is important to discuss because you must find techniques and practices that produce results for *you*. You must be able to assess what is working, what is real and when you are lying to yourself, and ultimately you must *know*—not think, but *know*—where you are and be able at some point to answer your own questions.

> The **only way** to progress
> is through your own direct experience.

This is the most important sentence in this section, and indeed in this book. Think on this for a moment. *The only way you progress is through your own direct experience.*

The best way to describe direct experience is to give you one. Look at the following picture.

There are two aspects of this optical illusion. Can you see them both? If not, keep looking at the picture until you do.

If you have seen this before, then you will have to think back and remember what it was like to see only one aspect, and then suddenly to see the other. They were both there, yet you didn't see it. At one point you didn't yet have the experience of it, and then you did.

What you learn about your true self is *exactly* like this. Even if someone *tells you* about it, even if they try to point it out to you, it is not your direct knowing through your own direct experience until it is. The efforts of others to help you to see are often referred to as *pointing*. Even though pointing may direct you to an awakening, it is still your awakening that happens through your own personal awareness. When it comes to waking up, if you don't see it yet, then you need to keep looking.

> You **CAN NOT** borrow the experience
> and understanding from others.

I mean by the term "borrowing" that some learning involves rote memorization and the ability to regurgitate the right answer. But being able to repeat the words others use is not a substitute for understanding and *knowing*. Nonetheless, many people would rather *appear* to know than do the work that leads to understanding.

There is little to be gained by borrowing the learning from others. It's not about memorizing the right answer, it's about directly knowing the answer. Many people see waking up as a medal of honor to be displayed. Since they see it as a prize, they are willing to cheat a little. The only person they are cheating is themselves.

It's not having the correct "words," it's about having the *experience*. The words themselves will not do. The piled-up words of others (including this book!) can only serve to point you towards something—and that is the *best* case. Borrowing the experience of others is pretending. If it's not your own direct experience, then it is an apparition, like Bigfoot or a UFO. You've heard about it, other people have talked about it, but it doesn't matter until you've seen and experienced it yourself. We are all still waiting to see a Bigfoot corpse and the remains of a crashed UFO.

> The best question you can ask yourself is,
> "What is my direct, true experience of this?"

The best question you can ask yourself is, "What is my direct, true experience of this?" Be forewarned, it probably won't be what you have been telling yourself it *should be*. By digging into your direct experience, you will find many instances where the reality of your experience is different from *the story* you are telling yourself about that experience. You will find many instances where your direct experience is different than what other people have been telling you it is or should be. Most people live in the story instead of in reality, and they accept this distortion as normal. Because of this, they don't look closely enough to find out what's really going on. The black box of their perception will remain the blind spot that they have lived with their entire lives.

> **DIY is Do-It-YOURSELF, not Do-It-With-Others.**

Note the question at the beginning of the last paragraph: The best question you can ask yourself is, "What is my direct, true experience of this?"

> Notice that the question is **not**,
> "What is everybody else's experience of this?"

Why is this important? First, you can't borrow it from others because if you do, then doubt will remain. Second, if you aren't sure how to discern if others are on the right path, then you may waste time on the wrong path. Third, not every method works the same for every person. And fourth, not everybody translates words in the same way. The ambiguity inherent in this work is unfortunate and can be frustrating because, like the optical illusion above, you only see it when you see it.

Groups often pop up around gurus and teachers. In the best case, the teacher has actually accomplished what is being taught. This teacher's students are often offended by the inflexibility of the teacher and seek someone who is "more their style." Often a group is a bunch of people hanging out and enjoying their shared delusion, the teacher included. Either way, at some point the teacher dies and then the students, who have not achieved what they came to achieve, begin to argue about what is what, what is the right approach, who is right and who is authorized to talk about it. This arguing comes from a place of mind and of self, perpetuating the mind and the self's attempts to stay in control, the opposite of what you are trying to accomplish.

At some point the group might become a religion. I see two large problems with this. The first is that religion is based around *belief* and not on direct experience. The second is that only those who are sanctioned to translate can tell you what's what. If you give this authority directly to the sheeple, then the ability to charge money for the instruction and inclusion, in perpetuity, is greatly diminished. Show me the religion that states that all people are good, although deluded and looking in the wrong direction, and that they are free and complete and whole in-and-of themselves. By adopting some new and different perspectives, they can free themselves of needless suffering from shame and guilt and low metaphysical value and lead prosperous, self-enhancing and, when appropriate, others-enhancing lives. They can directly experience their true nature and overcome the fears created by the mistaken belief in a separate self. So far I have not seen a single religion, and *very* few groups, with these organizing and operating principles.

The punchline is that you don't need a religion or a group or *anyone* to give you your birthright, because by definition you already have it!

Groups and organized religion are all too often looking east to see the sunset. It might be fun, there might be some nice people, but it seldom produces the results we are looking for. Only in the splinter groups of a few of these organizations have results been found—because they were insisting on finding out for themselves. They are the ones who secreted themselves away and looked west for the sunset while nobody else was looking.

Keep in mind what Groucho Marx famously said, "I don't want to belong to any club that would accept me as a member." This is good advice for most of this work.

***DO* it. Don't talk about it. Don't explain it. *DO* it.**

Talking about the previous optical illusion, the nature of pictures, discussing the existence of pictures and how the eyeball works, what it really "means"…none of this is the **DOing** of seeing the two aspects. This is just talking, measuring, labeling and assigning meaning…all parts of the mind, not what is beyond the mind. Notice what your experience was of recognizing the other aspect of the illusion. The realization and the *knowing* was there prior to the words in your mind.

For many of us, there is a strong desire to "figure it out" so we can understand. At times this contemplation produces some results and some glimpses, but at some point, it stops producing results and becomes a trap.

Talking about your experience and receiving instruction is helpful in finding your bearings and having some confidence that you are moving in the right direction. Keep in mind that your mind will want to stay in control, and that the process of measuring, comparing and labeling is itself the distraction that keeps you seeking and not finding.

Teachers

What is difficult, and where your discernment is needed, is figuring out what is working, how you know if it is working, and what to do next. Having others "point" you in the right direction is invaluable. Figuring out who these people are and how to use them can be tricky.

The best advice I can offer is to look for people who can propose specific techniques that lead to specific results. Focus on being a good student. Don't be surprised if a teacher ignores or dismisses you when you project your demands and expectations onto the work. Don't worship the teacher, just work the techniques and methods.

Remember that *mind* wants to run the show, so having people argue about things is just letting the mind stay in control. When people challenge those who are ahead of them, it is from the place of mind. So often teachers hear things like, "I just think that I feel that…" It is not reasonable to challenge someone's direct experience and knowledge of the next steps in this way. Actually, it is not a challenge at all, just the refusal to follow instructions. There is a path laid out, work those techniques and verify it for yourself. Keep in mind that your progress may not be as fast as you'd like. The mind is always offended at the work taken up to bypass the mind.

Chapter 31
You Don't Want This

What do you mean I don't want enlightenment? Of course I do! And what do you mean society doesn't want me to wake up?

Up to this point, making yourself into a work of art has consisted more of *adding* things to yourself and your life rather than *eliminating* things. It is similar to a body builder who works hard to add muscle. As you get more into this part of the path, you may notice that the work is more similar to that of a sculptor who whittles away at all that is NOT the final object.

Both of these examples imply that the base object can be improved through the addition of what's better and the elimination of what is not so good or helpful. It also implies a transformation over time—that at some point the destination is finally reached.

It is very important to note that these are *only metaphors* (i.e., onward and upward, more is better, a destination) we all live by, agree to and are taught from an early age. These metaphors are a part of our existential framework and we assign value and meaning from comparisons to these standards.

What you have read up to this point is based on the idea of the intrinsic value of the self and of the individual—which we state openly and without apology and which we celebrate fully (no religious guilt or sham moral asceticism here). To align with this, you must confront your fears, raise your standards, and commit to a path that seeks to maximize self-enhancing behavior to improve the probability of reaping the rewards from excellence.

Waking up takes a different direction from what we have discussed thus far. It also moves away from socially agreed upon values and metaphors. *It is for these reasons that you don't want enlightenment.*

From birth, you are raised by people who are not awake, and thus you are taught a perspective of the world that starts and ends with everyone as a separate individual, or separate *self*. This self needs constant improvement for fear of being "not-good-enough." As improvement happens, you get to be "better-than-average" and "better-than-others," which is a big improvement over "not-measuring-up." You are sold the idea of salvation, not just in religion, but in terms of the grand destination of finally being "complete, whole and finished." Perfection is the supposed guarantee against being excluded, unloved, hated, bullied, shamed. All the negative feelings (remember that for most people feelings are *proof)* that come with these human experiences seem to "prove" the initial assumptions that you have both an individual self and you must fix it to be good-enough. This in turn also provides proof that it is *possible* to be not-good-enough.

You have been programmed to adopt these metaphors, belief systems and the socially acceptable solutions. It is a game you are born into that has many layers of presuppositions that are predicated on faulty assumptions and conclusions. This leads to immense suffering. It is a game that cannot be won. It is a problem that cannot be solved from the level it was created on, which is the level of conceptual thought. Acquiring personal power and approaching personal mastery is the most helpful solution as viewed from the level of conceptual thought, and certainly from that perspective is far superior to the average life experience. Since you are starting on the level of that game, and it is self-enhancing to improve yourself and your life, then the version of the game you have been living out thus far makes perfect sense. At the level of waking up, the game isn't solved by winning it. The level of waking up solves the previous game by not believing in it.

You don't want enlightenment because it requires dropping the game, dropping winning and losing and dropping the destination. It requires dropping all hope and especially the hope of salvation.

Why would you want to drop all of *that?* Because as you start to drop it, you start to become free in a new way, and free in a way that can only be achieved by dropping. The *self* is invested in winning and by dropping the game you lose the chance to win. Almost everyone comes into this part of the work hoping to drop the loosing and keep the winning. This is the ultimate ego enhancement, and it is just a repackaged version of the *destination.* Waking up is about dropping the winning, the losing, the game and thus the self. Freedom does not come from winning the game—it comes from the absence of the game.

There is an old Zen saying, "Better not to start. Once started, better to finish." This refers to the process of waking up. At some point there are things you will see that cannot be unseen. Just like the optical illusion in the previous chapter, once you have seen both aspects, you cannot un-see them. The process of waking up and seeing reality is not always pleasant. Dropping things that you have held dear for so long may feel like a bully ripping them from your grasp. We are talking about something very close and dear to your heart—your *self*. Your hopes and dreams of finally "making it" and "getting there"— your longing for salvation and restoration that is built on your biggest, blackest fear—that you are fundamentally bad and not-good-enough.

> **The Zen saying serves as a warning, because those who have traveled this path far enough realized that enlightenment is not what you think it is going to be. It is *NOT* the improvement of yourself but rather an awakening into truths that supersede the need to be fixed or improved in the first place.**

> **Not Only Do *You* Not Want IT,**
> **Others Don't Want You to Have IT Either.**

As we have explored earlier, the process of gaining personal power can be disruptive to other people. Waking up is an extension of the disruption, despite how much others claim they want IT too.

To a regular person, with a distinct and separate self and the fragile ego that is a part of that self, coming face to face with someone who has awakened (or even partially awakened) is a slap to their ego. In "spiritual" circles, awakening is the ultimate attainment for yourself, and when others get there before you, it is the ultimate one-up on you. If you are making progress in your development, be prepared to be disliked and disbelieved. Be prepared for others to refuse to listen, to argue and attempt to project their preconceptions onto you.

The social upheaval of the 1960's is a great example of the fear that is generated when people stop behaving the way they are

The Path to Personal Power 167

"supposed to." When you stop believing in what you have been spoon fed, others fear that you may not want what they are dishing out and may prefer something else entirely—or nothing at all. Family values, religious beliefs, political affiliations, mom and apple pie are all at risk when you start to think for yourself.

LSD and Psilocybin mushrooms (among other psychedelic drugs) are currently Schedule 1 (i.e., illegal) drugs for a reason: they *work*. That is, they alter your perspective in a way very similar to the waking up process. Schedule 1 says that they have no beneficial effects, despite the fact that current research shows that the effects they have on your brain are similar to those of certain types of meditation. It would seem that the "authorities" are afraid of people thinking on their own, because when this happens they are harder to influence and control.

A byproduct of waking up is waking up to some social games and no longer playing them. The potential loss of membership and funding motivates the "authorities" to maintain the status quo and keep the sheeple in the dark…ready, willing and able to continue playing the games. Status quo is maintained by removing or discrediting the methods (psychedelics, in this example). Institutions and belief systems (e.g., governments and organized religions) cannot maintain power, authority and survive (let alone charge you for membership) if you don't believe in the problems they are trying to solve. As Osho famously said, "What would all the priests, politicians and therapists do if everyone got better? They'd have to commit suicide." (As a therapist myself, I will happily do something else for a living. For now, I'm not holding my breath.)

There are a lot of spiritual organizations and traditions that like to claim the "right" path and techniques. Scholars and gurus argue fine points and attempt to create maps of the territory. Waking up is not an academic exercise, but a personal experience. I strongly advise you take their words with a grain of salt. The best they can do is point you in a direction that sets you up to have your own experience. Keep in mind you aren't looking to experience more words, but something beyond that.

If at this point you still disagree with the title of this chapter and insist that you would like to wake up, be prepared to drop your preconceptions, your defense mechanisms and your favorite stories.

Chapter 32
The Great Paradox

You have spent your whole life looking at your *self,* attempting to improve your *self* and hiding aspects of your *self* from yourself and others. Now you are being asked to give **something** up so you can wake up.

What, pray tell, are you being asked to give up? You may remember the following from Christopher Hyatt's *Undoing Yourself with Energized Meditation and Other Devices*. It is included here (thank you, Original Falcon) to give you a hint.

TO KNOW ENLIGHTENMENT NOT TO JUST KNOW OF IT
A ZEN STATEMENT

You must give up the thing most precious to you.
    You must give up the thing which you love so dearly, the thing that you hold on to
—you must give it up—
—you must give it up.—

There can be no half-way measures in "finding"
    ENLIGHTENMENT.
It is not hiding anywhere.
It is HERE and NOW.

You must see that you are frightened,
that something is at STAKE all the time—
even in your dreams—something is at stake,
ALL THE TIME.

Everything which shocks you,
disrupts you, disturbs you, can be your friend.
Everything which allows you to sleep,
to be complacent
hinders you.

To become in Accordance with your
    TRUE POTENTIAL,
you must be in Discordance with yourself.
YOU ARE AT STAKE ALL THE TIME
    AND YOU LOOK FOR FOOD WHICH FEEDS YOU

Anything which delays your end——
    feeds you.
You digest this diet overabundant with FAT.
You are insatiable,
and require constant FAT to keep you going.
You use more energy and power maintaining
    THE ILLUSION
of your insatiable dream than Living.
You will even STRUT to death's window.

But to Know the DEATHLESS ONE—
you—**the strutter—must die.**
You must go on a diet—then
Starve to DEATH.
You must stop finding yourself in misery
in cranial pride,
—and historic stupidity.
You must stop strutting around like a fattened
    COW.
You must stop bowing down to your mistakes.
You must stop your idol worshipping.
You must surrender your misery.

You must stop acting surprised when
    something happens to you
FOR—it is the same old thing.
    You must stop reacting to things
    as you always HAVE.
You must stop proving your story.
    You must stop extending the past
    into the present and future.

You must stop defending your stupidity,
—YOUR SLEEP.
You must stop defending
YOUR MISERY.
YOU MUST WAKE UP

You even forsake your health to feed this Monster.
He drinks your blood,
this friend of yours.
You will sacrifice anything and everything to feed him.

Everyone and everything is food for you.
How people treat you (good-bad) is food for you.
You are so weak yet He is so strong.
Why do you prefer the insatiable one to HIM?

You oppose—you conform—all is food for you
You agree—you disagree—all is food for you.
You render opinions on this and that,
and spout authorities to back you up
—all is food for you.
You are surrounded by friends or you are alone—
all is food for you.
You are naked or adorned—
all is food for you.

The Path to Personal Power

SOMETHING IS **ALWAYS**
AT STAKE
SOMETHING IS ALWAYS ON THE LINE.
You strut around
proud of the misery
you have caused yourself.
You will do anything to preserve the misery.
You will fight,
you will sneer,
you will accuse,
you will blame,
you will steal, you will hide,
—all to preserve fear!
REMEMBER
THERE IS ALWAYS
SOMETHING
AT STAKE.
THAT SOMETHING IS YOU.

nothing can satiate
millions can not
fame can not
love can not
power can not
friends can not

ONLY ∞

AFTER YOU HAVE IT ALL THEN WHAT?

victories feed you
your failures feed you
your past feeds you
your ideas feed you
if your friends allow you to be complacent,
accept or like you, that is food for you.
If they hate you, that is food for you.

WHY ARE YOU SO HUNGRY?

Does death not even inspire your appetite?
Do you know death?
Or do you just have snapshots of it?
You act like you are immune from it,
that it just happens all around you
—but not to you.

Not even your own death can shudder you
move you from your—feeding frenzy.

WHAT FOOD IS NEXT?

Misery is food,
and you can find plenty of that.
You are never at a loss for that.

You never learn
because MISERY is food
You repeat the same mistake,
the same mistake,
the same misery
over and over.

Worst of all
you do it with pride.
with your sneer of superiority,
WITH A SENSE OF NEWNESS,
with a sense of uniqueness,
with a sense of choice,
or with a sense of helplessness.

Yet, it is the same mistake,
the same misery.

You do not even dare find a NEW MISTAKE
      A NEW MISERY

since that might wake you up from your
      FEEDING FRENZY

TECHNIQUE

When you speak to others notice your Dead phrases, and your patterned, stylized responses. They are indications that you are sound asleep. You have something at stake each time you repeat these habitual phrases and comments.

Find the patterned, machine-like phrases which you use over and over again and hold so dearly. Count the number of times you use them in a three-day period, and then:

STOP
STOP
STOP
STOP

Stay Awake
and each time you prepare to repeat
this DEAD TONE - - -

STOP

Say **Stop** to yourself.
Each time this stammered crippled phrase
rears Its Frightened head

STOP

BE SILENT.

Then, if you truly know who and what you are,

SAY IT SILENTLY

WAKE — — UP

Hyatt is referring to getting rid of your "self". From my research and experience, few people have understood what he was trying to say in this section. Or in the whole book for that matter, even though it is titled "Undoing YourSELF with Energized Meditation."

> **Great Secret #7**
> The Great Mysteries hide in plain sight.

Hyatt posits that the *self* is the cause of much pain and suffering and needs to be deprioritized and done away with. (Note: I mention Hyatt and this piece from *Undoing Yourself* because this was my introduction to the idea, and if you have read Hyatt's book this review may shed new light on its meaning as well as on the late author. And, since I'm writing for Falcon Press…)

Thus, the chapter name, The Great Paradox: you work hard for years to heal and develop *yourself,* and now you are being asked to get rid of your*self*. In all honesty, many people completely turn and run at this point. For some, it the most offensive thing they've ever heard. I recall a story Hyatt shared with me that Israel Regardie had told him. Aleister Crowley had looked into the Mahasatipatthana meditation, dropped it and never touched it again. Everyone is looking for the real deal and the Big Secret. When it doesn't meet their "occult needs" and their expectations, they are done.

Chapter 33
Turning Yourself In

How do you get rid of your *self*?

> The idea of getting rid of your *self* is the edge of a slippery slope. Once you start, you may find yourself quickly heading toward a point of no return. If you do not like points-of-no-return, stop reading!

At some point, you may realize for yourself what it means to get rid of your *self*. If you keep reading, and put some effort into it, and work the techniques, you may start getting the feeling that you are "onto something." Intuition will tell you that you are approaching a great truth, even before you understand it. This is because it is not something new, just something forgotten.

In my experience working with others, there is often a point where you both see it and don't see it at the same time, just for a moment. This is true when you are learning about your psychological patterns, defense mechanisms, hidden motivations and also about your true self. Even if you turn back at this point, you can't really say you don't know. You may not know fully, but you know something big is there. Just like the optical illusion earlier, there is split second of silent realization before you admit the other perspective and acknowledge it.

People struggle at this point because they are afraid. People get angry, disappointed, frightened, depressed or some combination of these because it isn't what they thought, or it doesn't meet their expectations or personal whims (the same can be said of the work in general). Once you know there is something behind this door, you are only lying to yourself if you continue to open other doors instead. For some people, finding doors instead of opening them is their preferred game. It is fun for the ego to continue to hunt for mysteries, and some would rather play-hunt than to catch and kill anything. At the end of the day, it's up to you.

The Path to Personal Power

> **How do you UnDo your *SELF*?**

You cannot get rid of yourself because you don't have a self. There is no *self*. There is no "I" or "me" inside, it is an illusion, and a very painful one.

> **Great Secret #1**
> There is no *SELF*.

> **There is no I, there is no ME, there is no separate individual self. Not now, not ever.**

The common response to this is "How can this be? What do you mean I don't have a "me" inside? I'm right here! Fuck you! This is bullshit!"

I understand if this is your reaction. You have been trained to look at the idea of your "self" since you can remember. You were taught to respond to your name, that you were separate and individual and unique. You were taught the great importance of this by people who have had no other perspective or experience of life. If you had a different perspective before this one had set up (like concrete), you probably don't remember it.

The fun part of all of this is that you can verify it for yourself. Why believe in believing and taking others' words for it?

> **No-Self is the ultimate punchline.**
> **It is the ultimate plot-twist…don't worry about it.**

Fear is the primary limiting factor in your journey at this point. Whenever fear arises and your mind goes into overdrive, you can contemplate the following fact. It will help immensely and allow you to re-ground yourself and carry on.

> **There is nothing to worry about, nothing to be afraid of, because what you are trying to do has always been the case. Nothing is gained or lost by seeing what has always been there, so there is NOTHING TO FEAR.**

We will dig into specific methods more as we go, yet I am discussing this upfront because it disarms the mind and begins to lower resistance.

Refer back to the optical illusion picture. It has the two aspects whether you see them or not. If that picture was sitting on a table for _____ number of years (fill in the blank with your own age), this would remain the case. YOU, like that picture, have an aspect that has been there just the same whether you have seen it or not. It is a fact that has been true all along, and this is the reason not to fear it or worry about it. Life has been happening and you have been going along with this truth in place, just overlooked. If this is the underlying truth, and it has been there all along...then what is there to worry about?

Might it be somewhat of a shock, a little unnerving? Yes. Does that mean your world is going to come to an end and you will lose everything? No. What your mind tells you, and what you can learn to experience for yourself are *COMPLETELY DIFFERENT*. Truth doesn't need your incessant mental chatter for it to be truth. In fact, the mental chatter is what is in between you and your realization of your truth.

I use the words *realization of the truth* because my telling you the punchline is ***NOT*** the same as your seeing it and, therefore, knowing it for yourself. I can tell you there are two aspects, but it is up to you to experience it for yourself. All of the discussion about not borrowing another's experience was said in preparation for this point. You have to do your own work. And until you do, you do not know it, nor can you say it's bullshit because you don't see it.

There are two big questions that spring up around the work of waking up. The first is, "**What** is it? **What** are we hoping to gain or accomplish by waking up?" The second question is, "**How** do we come to see this for ourselves? **How** do we make this happen?"

No-Self is one of the big **"Whats"** of awakening. There are a few other "whats," and depending upon your frame of reference and your practice you may come across these as well. If there is no self, then there is no agency, which means that "you" are not the doer of any actions. If there is no separate self, then the illusion of other objects being separate from oneself can disappear. All of these experiences have a name in Zen parlance, but keep in mind that labeling, talking and arguing about them doesn't produce results or understanding.

The Path to Personal Power

The *"Hows"* that we use to bring about the awakening consist of methods and experiments—in other words, "things to do"—that bring about the changes. Fortunately the methods have been Westernized, corroborated and are being scientifically researched.

It is often said that the mind, or ego, does not wish to go quietly to turn itself in. It is a great illusion that carries with it much power and energy. It is also the source of a tremendous amount of suffering. As you unwind this structure, you regain that wasted energy and suffer less. As you start to have glimpses into your true nature, you will most likely feel a sense of relief, unburdening, peace as you move away from the drama and the story of you.

It is worth mentioning that I can only write from my own experiential perspective and discuss what has worked for me and others I know. It is not my intention to catalogue all of the aspects and avenues of practice, as this would require many books. My intention is to provide you an expedient way to navigate the darkness and open a few doors to awakening.

Some may debate that coming out with the answer, going straight to the "what" up front is "throwing pearls before the swine." Maybe so, but in my opinion that is old thinking and a defense mechanism used by those who haven't awakened yet themselves. If this truth hides in plain sight, then it will continue to do so even if I tell you what it is. In my estimation the punchline serves as motivation to do the work, instead of blindly sitting on a cushion and hoping for something to happen.

Why share this at all?

The more people who get it, the more this whacked out species can evolve beyond politics, violent religion and "human" nature, and the better this world becomes—for me and like-minded individuals—to live in.

Chapter 34
The Overlay

Looking into what I call *the overlay* is both a fact **and** a method. It helps to provide a foundation that can speed up your progress, as this is also part of what you are trying to see. It is also one of the ways to overcome the fear and resistance that may arise during this part of the work.

Earlier we were looking into the fact that the conceptual world rests on top of and obscures the real world, like thick fog gets in the way of our ability to see things clearly. By looking into this further, we can establish some solid ground on which to stand to help us progress in this part of the path.

We discussed earlier how "the map is not the territory" and the description is not the object. All you need to do is apply this thinking to the idea of *you, the "idea" of your SELF*. Is your self-description of the object (you), the object? If you work in this direction you will discover that all you can experience about the words that describe (and point to) the "self" are more words about the self.

Thought is not in real time; it is always after the fact. It is always after direct experience. It is about the recalled past, about an imagined future. Present moment awareness is part of the practice. If you are fully in the moment, you will see the gap between direct experience and when mind comes after to talk about it.

Thought is not an accurate reflection of reality. There is plenty of research into our thinking errors and biases that show how we not only distort the present moment, but our memories as well. There is current research that shows that our own actions take place well before our brain registers them and comments on them. The arm was already moving towards the coffee cup *before* we have the internal words that say "reaching for the cup."

The thinking about a thing is not that thing. Thought contains labeling, definitions, stories, excuses…but not the "thing in itself."

Thoughts do not contain "you" either. Think deeply on that. If your thoughts are not you, are you your thoughts, or is there something else?

> **All thought is an overlay on top of reality.**

Transparencies were a technology used for teaching when I was in school. They were clear pieces of plastic which could be written on or printed on. The teacher could have things printed onto the transparencies, lay them onto the projector which would project them onto a screen. Multiple transparencies could be stacked, and they could be written on with a magic marker. You might have a human skeleton on one transparency, then you could take a second transparency and lay it over the top of it, perhaps one with the names of the bones on it.

View your thoughts as an overlay on top of reality, like a transparency over a picture. In this way you can view the world as seen through the direct experience of your senses, *and* see your thoughts as the overlay. As you understand this perspective, thoughts (along with concepts and beliefs) are seen to be less real. They are infinitely less important than the direct experience.

Experiment: Look out the window. You see things out there in the world, but you do not see the glass. Take an erasable marker (careful here) and write the names of what you see on the glass. Tree. Bird. Car. Obviously the names are not the things you see, nor are they attached to them in any way, other than as an equivalence that you have created in your mind. Erase those words then look up the Sanskrit words for tree, bird and car and write those on the window. Are the tree, car and bird now those words? Erase that, and then write on the window the words "memories of the past," "thoughts about the future," "successful" and "depressed." We are getting a little more abstract, and you have to reference your internal experience for all of these, as they are not "here" in real time. What if instead of the glass you could write these words on your eyeglasses or contact lenses, or better yet, your eyeballs?

Having a thought or belief about something is not bad in itself, but the average person lives almost entirely in the thought space, which causes all kinds of inaccuracies, distortions, "bogeymen" and therefore great levels of undue suffering. It is very similar to being afraid of a scary shadow. If you don't understand that a shadow isn't real, then you are going to spend a lot of life energy on it instead of on something worthwhile. I look at all psychological "problems" in this manner.

Thoughts don't make reality real. Neither do words, whether spoken or written. Thoughts about what you really are do not make you real, they obscure what you are. Thoughts are like clouds. They do not define the sky and the vastness of space—they obscure it.

What is the importance? If you are thinking that you are one way or another…then drop those thoughts and learn to *look*. A large chunk of meditation is learning how to look without getting distracted.

> **Thinking creates maps, labels, categories, concepts, equivalencies…. reducing reality to just piles of words, into self-narrated internal movies.**

People are constantly referencing their internal experience, their map of "what it is and what it means." They often reference this *more* than they reference present-moment reality.

> If the mind (overlay) is telling you what's what
> that you are going to be in pain
> that you are at risk of losing everything
> that nothing will be sweet or worthwhile again
> that you will never have fun or feel love again

AND…

> **The more you believe this crap in your head,
> the more you feed the "thoughting,"
> the more your emotions are tweaked,
> the harder it is to progress.**

> The mind is telling you this through thoughts (lies)
> It is a story overlaid on top of your direct experience
> To the point of brainwashing you
> Keeping your direct experience,
> Your truth,

Almost completely unknown to you
As if a blanket was laid on top of a flower garden

Your thoughts want to stay in charge.

Your *thoughts* watch other thoughts, it's not you watching other thoughts…seek to *see this*. Close your eyes and watch for a while. Thoughts drift by, other thoughts talk about those, and still others talk about the talking. Then a thought comes along and says, "See, this is both real and important." It's the last lie that makes the whole chain ***true?*** The last lie makes all lies real, true and important. Then you have a feeling which, if you remember, makes it **proven reality.** It must be real if a thought says it is and triggers an emotion! You can lay back, close your eyes and **watch this.**

WAKE UP!

A story about a story on top of a story until sleep comes. Or death. Why not wake up to this before you die, and enjoy peace while still alive?

Mind wants to preserve the illusion, and it will attempt to scare you away from dropping thought and just simply being in the moment.

Think about how many moments are spent in thought and story, labeling and having preferences, and then more stories about all of this. Now think about the ratio of these moments to ones without thought, just simply being in the moment. That momentum and habit is your ***karma***.

If all thought is an overlay, then the contents of thought may not be so important. A mental "warning light" on the mental dashboard may not signal any problem, in fact it might be wired in reverse or randomly. An example of this is the thought, "Is this person mad at me?" Some people think everyone is mad at them and it's because they are a bad person.

Your thoughts tell you things about other thoughts and feelings. Thoughts jump in to tell you about your direct experience to the point you barely recollect direct experience. The present moment is spent in thought. The current cultural fascination with zombies is embarrassingly ironic.

Asleep at the wheel...

Loosening the ties of conceptual thought will help your insight and meditative practices. It is a great start that sets you up for progress as well as a great reminder to keep you on track.

Chapter 35
Methods

Methods are what we can do to produce awakening. While there are many methods, I prefer Direct Path flavors, because it suits my impatient temperament. As far as I'm concerned, methods are not designed to support belief systems and group conformity—they are meant to produce results.

Before getting started, I think that it is useful and important to separate the methods from the cultures and belief systems they come from. This helps save you time, frustration and dead ends.

Much of the discussion on enlightenment comes from *religious* traditions. Buddhism, Theravada, Advaita and so on, have traditionally been the primary sources of discussion on enlightenment. The problem with these traditions are the beliefs that must be accepted and the codes of conduct that must be followed.

Stages, levels, experiences and in what order they are experienced, descriptions of exact experiences, and attempts to validate the exactness of your experience so you can figure out what "level" you are on…almost all of this is noise and distraction.

Different rules and codes of conduct are espoused. What you eat, how and if you have sex, what you abstain from…none of this has much impact on what you are trying to accomplish. Do these rules exist outside of thought? Is there a "higher power" that exists outside of thought and is judging you?

A lot of good thought and pointers come from the original systems, but the adherence to the "doctrines" seems misplaced. One example is the wheel of rebirth and past lives. If there is no self, what is it that would be carried from life to life? Since the conceptual self exists only in thought, you would only be left carrying memories of other lives forward. This is like remembering a dream—which is equally unreal because it is not present NOW. Considering how multiple lives would work, or how to develop that power is in the realm of thinking, and thus a fantasy distraction point. People spend a lot of time trying to remember past lives and feeling bad that they can't do it—instead of spending time on something that produces real results. It may be that the "endless cycle of rebirths" was referring to each moment of forgetting between each moment of remembering, thus creating a multitude of "lives" for us each day. Each episode of forgetting brings with it a *metaphorical* birth back into suffering again. What remains in front of you is your own direct experience and your own work to do *in the present moment.*

Religions of the east are no different than religions in the west. Religions are about *believing* in things. Believing is a product of thought. Thought is an overlay on top of reality. Why believe in believing? Even if the beliefs are nice and pleasant, they are not as nice and pleasant as your underlying reality.

> Why believe in believing?

The most commonly used word used to label the goal of waking up is **Enlightenment.** This word is loaded with preconceptions and platitudes—statements like "the end of all suffering." It is best to drop all that you have heard and instead of trying to define and understand this as an end state, look to the practices for your own experience. Keep in mind that you cannot preconceive of what you have not yet experienced. It is illogical and a waste of time to be comparing your experience to your preconceptions.

There is a subset of Zen Buddhism that looks at a more immediate approach to realization. This is often called *Direct Path.* This approach differs from "gradual path" techniques because it actively uses thought and contemplation to undo thought itself. Traditional seated meditation is not always the most useful place to start, although it is the most popular. After I had more direct experiences of silence and of No-Self, it became easier for me to sit. I felt less frustration around trying to "stop" thinking, ruminating on the purpose of sitting, and wondering when something was going to happen.

There is a common misconception that since our true nature is already whole and complete and one with everything, there is no practice or doing required. This is a lazy and irresponsible idea propagated by people who want to claim knowing without having done the work required to *know*. This is certainly not a Direct Path shortcut. This may be the ultimate example of "knowing of" without having any direct experience of this fact. Our completeness may in fact be "true," but until you have the direct experience of this, the words do not help and only serve to give *premature* enlightenment.

> **There is something to *do* until there is no more self to do things.**

There are multiple ways to go about your practice, and what I'm presenting to you is *one* way. These methods have worked for me and others with whom I've worked. I suggest you explore them, work with them, and note what seems to work for you. Keep in mind that even if something doesn't seem to work now, it may work later, so revisit different methods from time to time.

Developing the Observer

In all that you do while you are awake, can you see that there is an observer to your doing? When you catch your reflection in a mirror, there is a slight sensation of, "Oh, there I am!" Then you return to your normal sense of aloofness. This is similar to driving somewhere and not remembering if the stoplights were red or green. You just weren't there. This low level of awareness—being lost in things—is not what you are looking to cultivate.

You develop the observer by remembering that you have one. The more you can develop a sense of *remembering,* the more you can bring yourself back to the present moment and the less you are lost in your head.

As an experiment, stop reading for a moment and ask yourself this question: How many times while reading this book have I thought "Hey, I _____(insert your name) am reading this book!"? Is reading just happening, or is there a part of you that knows that *you* are reading? I'm guessing this level of remembering could easily happen a *lot* more often.

Another experiment: while watching a movie seek to remember that you are watching a movie. You are watching it, and awareness is aware that *you* are watching it. How often do you remember that, "I am watching this movie"? An entire movie can roll by without this awareness ever coming into play (or an entire lifetime if you are not careful).

You can expand *remembering the observer* in many of the activities that you do on a daily basis. Washing the dishes and other chores are great places to do this. Taking a shower, getting dressed, driving, exercising, working, etc.

There are some interesting things that you can take away from doing this. One is that it helps to insert a pause in your reactions. It can change a knee-jerk reaction into an *actively chosen, wise-minded response.* Think about the implications of this when having a tense or heated discussion with someone. What about behaviors that you want to avoid, such as overeating or other habits? This is a very useful and effective skill to have, in addition to its helping you to wake up.

As you practice, you will find that over time you remember more and more frequently. This means less time lost in your story and drama and thought, and more time spent *in the present moment.*

The flip side of this experiment is also extremely useful. Look deeply (this is a *contemplation*) into the idea that while you are NOT there, life is happening all by itself quite effortlessly. If this is the case, do *YOU* really need to be there at all? Apparently, most things in your life happen without there being a *self* to make each and every decision. You are sitting somewhere reading a book, and all of a sudden you remember, "Hey, I'm reading this book!" and then you further realize that *you* weren't there just a moment before that. Maybe that *you* doesn't need to be there after all.

Don't be angry at yourself for not being aware of the observer at all times. Each time you become aware, your brain notices the difference and learns *from the **difference**,* not just the successes. You can learn a lot by observing the differences between these levels of awareness and contemplating the points I've mentioned. Remember, you are looking to experience the realizations around these experiments for *yourself,* not just take my word for them.

Mindfulness

The previous exercises were methods of mindfulness around the observer. This method can be expanded further when you mentally *note* all of your sensory experience. It then is no surprise that this technique is often called *noting*.

If you have studied Dr. Hyatt's UnDoing methods you will see that he references the earliest version of this technique which is called Maha-satipatthana. He also called this the *You Meditation* or *Sensing and Feeling*. This is a meditation that has you focusing on your sensory experience in the moment. The *You Meditation* can be practiced both at the end of UnDOing sessions and on its own.

While sitting or reclining (or doing anything for that matter), you simply "notate" to yourself what is going on in your sensory experience. Examples are:

Sight: There are colors. There are shapes. There is tingling in the eyes. There are tears in the eyes.

Hearing: There is a bird singing. There is the sound of a paper bag being crumpled. There is the sound of my breath.

Smell: There is freshly cut grass. There is the ocean.

Taste: There is sour, bitter, sweet.

Feeling: There is my arm, foot. (Becoming aware of different body parts.) There is tingling in my leg. There is twitching in my face.

From the body you can progress to the mind.

Exercise: Sit or lie down with closed eyes. Focus on the darkness, the emptiness. When a thought comes along, say to yourself "thinking." Have an attitude as if the thoughts were trying to sneak up on you, and that by saying "thinking" you are letting it know you see what it is up to so that it retreats. Don't have an expectation to produce a result other than to create space for your presence and content-free awareness.

You can then progress to emotions and moods. Are you aware of your moods, or only influenced by them? Moods and emotions are often justification for behavior. Becoming aware of your moods, acknowledging them and not using them to justify behavior can be very beneficial in your life.

Osho summarizes mindfulness simply, "Be watchful of your body, then watchful of your mind, then watchful of emotions and moods. Remember one thing, meditation means awareness. Whatever you do with awareness is meditation."

Contemplation

Contemplation involves simply going inside and looking into things in a deliberate, focused way. When your mind drifts bring it back to the subject of contemplation.

I like contemplation as a method because it allows us to use our natural tendency to problem solve, and our desire to figure things out and learn. As a method it seems to be well suited for the western mind.

You can approach contemplation the same way you approach learning and having new experiences. Look to *experience the learning* for yourself. At some point you were taught how to count. You have two apples, and you add two more apples to those and now there are…four. At some point in this process something clicked and it became *your experience* of four. At this point there was no more use to "believe" in four, it was your understanding and experience for yourself. Another example is the optical illusion a few chapters back. I pointed out that there are two ways to look at it. You looked for this until you *saw* it for yourself. This is how you should approach contemplation to get results.

The examples above describe *pointing,* which is another Direct Path term. The subject of contemplation is the optical illusion, and the teacher points you to look for the two ways to see it. The teacher points to what is known and helps you to see it for yourself. The resulting understanding comes from seeing it yourself.

Choosing subjects to contemplate should be done in terms of understanding what you hope to learn. Teachers can provide enormous benefit in this way, in that they know how to produce a certain result.

Let's use a poor beginner's choice of subjects to start with, an old and popular Zen koan for contemplation:

"Two hands clapping makes a sound. What is the sound of one hand clapping?"

Try it for yourself. Close your eyes, clap your hands in front of you, notice the sound. Now just swing one hand in front of you as if you were clapping with one hand. What is the sound? It should be obvious that there is no sound. But what is the point being made? What is hoped that you will learn and experience for yourself? These are difficult questions to answer for a beginner.

Here are a few pointers to help you along, which you can use as an experiment. Take a few minutes with each of these questions as a *subject of contemplation*. Again, close your eyes and clap with one hand and bring one of these questions with you. What is your experience of *looking to experience the sound of no-sound?* What is your experience of the silence? Who is listening for the sound? Are you separate from the silence? The *experience* of the answers to these questions is the point, and it is not a superficial point at all.

The value of the koan and the subject is not easily uncovered without some help. Also, understanding that you are not separate from the one-everything or that your true identity may be silence, for example, are not quick and easy understandings to experience. Most beginners would give up on that long before they *saw* what the contemplation points them to see. If you look up the meaning of the koan on the internet you will find a lot of answers. Each one of these ideas, like the ones I have provided, can be their own subject of contemplation.

Much of what you have read in this book so far can and should be a source of contemplation. You can contemplate the idea of metaphysical value—it is possible that it's impossible to be "bad"?

Contemplate the overlay. Deliberately watch the mind come along and label your experiences *after* they have happened.

Contemplate your own awareness. Where does it go when you sleep? How do you have awareness focus back on its own source?

Jiddu Krishnamurti often asked his audience big questions, such as "Is it possible for time to come to an end?" The best way to interact with his and similar material is to contemplate this yourself, not just read and collect the questions. When you are fully in the present moment, does time exist or is it a concept? Does your awareness age or have an age? How do you know that time is passing? Does time exist without the story you tell yourself about it existing?

Ramana Maharshi liked to use the single question "Who Am I?" One can also use "where" and "when" am I? The simple question "Who am I?" can bring about quite a bit of change. Some have said that this one question can bring you all the way.

No-Self

Seeing No-Self is its own special contemplation. When you use the words "self" or "I" or "me", what do these words reference? Is it your body? Is it your thoughts that are "you"? You are so certain there is a "self" in there, a unique "you", but have you ever really seen it? How do you know that you have a self? You **tell yourself that this is so.** But is your *self* the thoughts about yourself, or is there something else? Or nothing else?

Seeing No-Self is something that you can see for yourself if you are so inclined. Why would you want to do this? There are two common answers. The first is that you want to wake up and are willing to go all the way to understand your true nature. The second is that you suffer more than you like and you want to be free of this. In my case both were motivating.

Think about the city or town you live or grew up in. There is probably a town sign (e.g., "Chicago") at its edge. What does that sign actually refer to? Is every blade of grass and every bird "Chicago"? Is every person "Chicago"? How do you know where it begins and ends? Chicago is a concept of a space, a place on a map. When you point to the map and say "That's Chicago" what does this really mean?

Similarly, when you ask yourself the question "Who am I?" what is the answer? Is the answer "I'm *ME!*"? Go inside and find the me. Can you find this "I" or "me" *outside of the inner story that keeps telling you that "of course it's there"*? You may find for yourself that your *self* cannot be found outside of the self-referencing story. You may find that "self" only exists as part of the conceptual overlay. Write the word "me" on a mirror and look into it. If "that's not it," then what is?

Once No-Self is seen, what feeds the flywheel of self and ego is reduced and momentum will continue to decrease with practice.

It is infinitely easier to work on your direct experience of No-Self than to argue about it and discuss it round and round. It is not an academic idea—it is a fact that you can verify for yourself. It is the same as the optical illusion presented earlier. Both aspects are there, whether you see it or not. No-Self is also there. It is so—whether you see it or not. It is a fact that this is different from what you have been told and what you have experienced so far in your life.

Vipassana

Vipassana is traditional seated meditation where many people start their journey. This can be done by itself, but it's a slow route. Sitting on a cushion while attempting to watch my breathing and trying not to have thoughts did not produce much for me other than frustration—at least in the beginning. This is why I've started by sharing what I have found to be much more expedient. (Note to longtime cushion sitters: don't be offended if there are more expedient ways of getting results. There's no point continuing to preserve a poor investment.)

Sitting and watching your breath keeps your awareness on one of your sensory doors—in this case feelings—as in feeling the breath in and out. By focusing on that primary, in-the-moment experience, you are taking focus away from thoughting and being somewhere else other than in the moment. You can see how this is similar to the *noting* (mindfulness) practice. Keep in mind that this practice is not to become a trance, but to stay actively aware and in the moment.

Note: I found Vipassana easier and more productive later in my practice than in the beginning because I was more familiar with silence and how to pay attention to it. It is easier to use space or silence as an object of attention if you know what you are looking for.

Reading and Journaling

Reading and rereading things that add to your awareness helps to reinforce what you are working on. This deepens your understanding as you review the steps from being asleep to being more awake.

Journaling and keeping notes of the things that create little shifts is helpful. It gives you a place to store your nuggets of learning. You have to work hard at times to up your awareness, so there is no point to letting your good work slip away and be forgotten. You should journal all of your other techniques, what works and where you get stuck. Writing in itself is a great method of learning and reinforcing.

Chapter 36
Cultivation

I like the verb "to cultivate," as in "cultivating understanding." We can look at bringing about enlightenment in terms of bringing about a tomato plant. You work to prepare the ground, turning it over and adding nutrients to the soil. You till a furrow, you plant the seed and cover it with soil. You plant it in conditions where the weather is suitable for its growth. You water it, and over time it does what seeds do...it sprouts. Once you see the sprout, you know that something is happening. If the sprout continues to be nourished by the soil, the sun and water, it matures. Once the fruit is fully matured and ripe, you can enjoy it as well as extract seeds from it and plant them.

You do not need religion and a belief system to bring this about; it is natural and organic. You *do* need a seed, soil, sun, water and proper temperatures. You also need instructions and guidelines. The experience of others who have produced a "sprouting" or a full-grown plant can help you to understand what is working, what may not be working, and to answer questions that serve as a distraction to either your work or your life.

Figuring out that *not* planting the seed under a bush or in a pile of leaves is helpful to not waste time and effort. Figuring out that you had squash seeds and not tomato seeds is good to know. Understanding what the sprout looks like is nice to know, in case that is a little green weed popping up, giving you premature hope.

The rules and guidelines can be communicated from one person to another, provided you understand two important points. The first is that there are many people who have never grown a tomato yet collect information, memorize the words of others, and then become armchair experts. These people puff their ego and demonstrate their self-importance by telling you what's what when they don't know. (This is more widespread than you think, leaving you a giant pile of crap to sift through. The purpose of this book is to eliminate that pile as best we can.) The second point is that my tomato grew in my garden in my yard in my hometown. Your seed, soil and conditions are different, so the guidelines are *more approximate* than any of us would like, but they will have to do because every situation is unique. I may insist on a shortcut, use a special type of water, and be certain that *that* was the key, but in fact that might be the key *in my experience* and not translate to you. It may be my *thoughts* around what worked for me, and therefore my preferred method, but it's hard to be absolutely sure it will translate to you. Thus, I can provide options in a range of possibilities, and you can look for solutions that seem to be best-fits for you. Because you don't have a sprout yet, it's not easy to determine what to do next, and you have to look at a large amount of information that may or may not work. Things to consider…

The Soil: Your body.
- Yoga, UnDoing work, physical strength and health. Eliminating chronic tension and emotional armoring.

Conditions: Your life.
- Mental health, absence of psychological distress and distractions, not hating yourself, not resisting the facts of life.
- Not consumed by worry around biological survival and money.

Work: What needs to be done to sprout the seed and mature the plant.
- Philosophical understanding: understanding the difference between unmediated reality and the conceptual world (this could be a condition *and* work to be done)
- Getting yourself in order
- Getting your life in order

The Seed: Your awareness.

The Sun: Proper meditation techniques that bring the temperature up and bring about the sprouting. The better the techniques, the better the light and the better the growth.

The Science of Cultivation

Recent years has seen some exciting research that relates to the cultivation of "enlightenment." While my tomato plant metaphor is nice, scientific research into neurology and brain function brings our understanding of meditation and its effects out of a dark age. This is significant because it allows us to understand what causes (meditation, psychedelics) to create what effects (specific decreased brain activity), thereby taking much myth and guesswork out of the pursuit while lending credibility to the practice and hope to practitioners.

Meditating on a cushion with the hopes that someday something good will happen takes too much blind faith for most people. Instruction around meditation has often been vague due to translation from foreign texts and distant cultures. It has also been difficult to weed out the religion, moral platitudes, cultural mores and myth. Now we can drop all of that and get straight after it.

Recent research in neuroscience has given some great models and explanation of what's going on in our brain around mystical experiences. In 2001, neurologist Marcus Raichle first used the term "default mode" to describe the brain's resting state functioning. The Default Mode Network, or DMN is a large-scale brain network highly correlated for specific functions, such as thinking about oneself, others, right and wrong, status, the past and the future. This network has also been called the task-negative network because it tends to turn off when one is focused on a specific task, shifting that process to the task-positive network.

The DMN is responsible for one's sense of *self*. As you ponder the functions of the DMN, you can think of the byproducts of this network activity—worry and anxiety—because thinking about changes in status, being right or wrong, remembering the past and thinking about future outcomes generally cause those feelings. It turns out that the default mode of our brain is not just a neutral *idle*.

When the DMN is deactivated, you have a potential range of states from concentration, flow states and mystical experiences. MRI and PET scans have shown that meditation and psychedelic drugs both disable the DMN, correlating to classical mystical experiences.

There is a consensus among some researchers and meditation practitioners that is worth noting. Direct Path techniques of meditation such as direct inquiry and contemplation show the brain a different and preferable state to the default mode because it is more peaceful and uses less energy. The brain learns through the comparison of default mode to the peaceful state where the default mode is inactive. With each repetition of a pause or silence, the brain begins to change and optimize for less default mode, even though you may not be aware of this taking place.

The stronger the experience of silence when the default mode is inactive, the greater the effect can be to changing both your brain and your perception of the experience. Both meditators and those who have taken psychedelics claim the experiences to be transcendental, more real than normal reality and more important personally. Because each repetition and experience changes the brain permanently to some extent, leads me to think that the claims that these experiences are lifechanging goes beyond perception and anecdotal evident to *actual and lasting neurological change.* This is also my personal experience.

Starting meditative techniques with an understanding that there is a small cumulative change for the better, certainly can give you a solid understanding of *why* it's a good idea as well as *how* it works. Knowing that Direct Path methods produce these results by creating spaces of silence in the mental chatter of the DMN, even if not a quick fix, can help you persist knowing that something is happening for the better. Knowing that certain chemicals also can create profound and lasting positive neurological change also gives you a different perspective on why these have been important in certain tribal and religious ceremonies for thousands of years.

I encourage you to reflect on the conceptual focus of the Default Mode Network and the correlation this has with much of the material presented in this book. Think back to imaginary problems, the black box, the pipe that is not a pipe, Escher's endless looping stairs. Think about what humans will do to protect their beliefs and concepts. Think about being a rebel and not playing the game that your *self*—and everyone else's *self*—is playing.

> Drop the DMN, Drop the self, Drop the rest of the concepts.

Further Resources and Reading

How Enlightenment Changes Your Brain, Dr. Andrew Newberg
Stealing the Fire, Steven Kottler and Jamie Wheal
Gary Weber Blogspot

Chapter 37
Dealing With Difficulties

> **Great Secret #∞:**
> The nature of your true identity,
> without having a self,
> has always been this way,
> whether you were aware of it or not.

It is useful to talk about getting unstuck before it happens. Doing this acts as an inoculation *before* you run into trouble, so that if and when the time comes you have some resources available to you.

First off, looking into No-Self and other aspects of waking up can be unsettling. The ego/self, although it does not exist outside of the story of itself, is there for a reason. At some point the creation of the reflective "self" or ego must have been an evolutionary decision that made sense in our past. In that case, there is a pragmatic and protective function to it. It is trying to protect its own agenda, which is the biological imperative: procreation and replication of the gene pool. This goal is not necessarily aligned with the personal goal of power we have been exploring. Thus, our attempts to displace the "self" from its ruling throne are met with resistance.

Your "self" will attempt to dissuade you primarily through fear. It will create the necessary thoughts and internal dialogue to create fear, sadness, depression and anxiety to steer you away from your efforts. Since emotions are proof of reality for most people, they do not push past these phantom sirens of doom. Knowing that this is going to happen before it happens helps you to best deal with it when it does. Think of it as a map to your inner haunted house. If you know ahead of time that a ghost is going to pop out at a certain point, it is much less influential when it does.

Anxiety and fear will arise as you challenge your deeply held social and familial programming. Most of what you have been led to believe is inaccurate or wrong. This is not easy to accept, as no ego wants to admit it has been so wrong for so long. It is a direct frontal assault to your ego, which has been telling you how smart, right and special you are for your entire life. Few want to give up this fantasy for progress in the real world.

Waking up and working with No-Self may create fears of ceasing to exist. Fear of losing all love, fun and happiness may also arise.

Some reminders that may help you with this are:

- Remember that those who have passed through the final gate report the opposite of these fears and tell you not to worry about it at all. They did not die, they report that their feelings of love and acceptance are much greater. They report that their creativity and productivity are also enhanced.
- The nature of your true identity—having no "self"—has always been the case. It has been this way since you were born. As this is the underlying truth (lying beneath a scary story), then you are simply becoming reconnected with this truth.
- Remember that the "feelings" of fear do not mean there is anything in reality to be afraid of. You need to see for yourself that the tiger is in your head and not in your room. You will often find that life's limitations and boundaries are only in your mind.
- Life does itself whether or not there is (or you think you are) a controller of it. Losing the controller doesn't matter. Is the controller always there? What happens during all the time in a day that you forget to be the controller and forget to take credit and ownership for all that you think you do? Life does itself while you sleep, and the self and controller disappear.

Maintaining a balanced life, eating and sleeping regularly, and developing a selfcare routine that takes into consideration the demands of this work will help greatly.

It is important to allow yourself to be and let the work you are doing settle in. The work cannot be forced or put into a timetable. Each person is unique and how much and how quickly you can push depends on many factors. Attempting to force progress will result in unnecessary delays and lead to burnout and possibly emotional instability. Learning is taking place on a neurological level, not just on a mental one, and that process only goes so fast. Remember, the rule is to *make haste slowly.* If the work becomes self-diminishing you are to stop and reset.

Be careful in comparing yourself to other people and their experiences. What happened for them—in what order and how long it took—is unique to them. It will not help if you get caught up in comparisons and put pressure on yourself. When you get frustrated, ask yourself questions like "Who is upset? Who is behind? Who determines these things?" In this way you can turn difficult emotional states into learning opportunities.

Take the descriptions of the experiences of others with a grain of salt. There are people who have had mystical and awareness/insight experiences without really doing much to bring them about. Eckhart Tolle says that he just woke up different one day after being extremely depressed. When someone like this attempts to describe what happened, what they did and what you need to do and/or understand, it may not make sense. It may not make sense to the general population, but for some people who are in the right spot it may be very helpful. Glean what you can and move on. Don't get stuck trying to figure out someone else's map if it doesn't work for you.

Be very careful around peak states and experiences. As you progress, you may have insights, transcendent moments and profound moments of clarity. Mystical experiences and serendipities may also happen. The best way to handle these is to acknowledge and accept them, not dwell on them, and continue on with your practices.

The goal of the work is not to have and collect peak experiences, but to create a lasting transformation and state. Focusing on peak experiences is an easy trap because the ego wants to be special, more "advanced" than others and collect points for its accomplishments. Real progress is not only about peak states and, because of this, is less appealing to the ego.

If you get enamored with peak experiences, you will be forever trying to regain and reexperience the peak states instead of making real progress. This subtle mindset also keeps you in a perpetual state of "what I once had and now have lost," which is detrimental to progress. That heavy mood is not the curious, accepting and joyful mood that you should seek to have as you practice.

Another thing to note is that peak experiences also create a dependency and over-focus on the tool that created them. For example, if you had a big experience because of a hallucinogen, you will focus on that tool and tend to discard others. Your brain needs exposure to many different methods, and you won't know which one it will need next. A good analogy is working your way through a large mansion with many locked doors. Just because one key on the keyring worked once doesn't mean it will open any more doors and allow you to progress. You never know which key will work, when it will work, how many times it will work and what order the keys are in.

Frustration and disappointment are the byproducts of expectations. You cannot be disappointed with your real-life experience if you aren't comparing them to "what you think should be happening" and "what happens with others." Drop all expectations and preconceptions. Most of what you have read about waking up is overhyped and glorified, and often written by people who have not done the work or achieved the results. Asking yourself "who is complaining and missing out?" and similar self-inquiry questions can help with frustration and a lack of patience. If there is a "self" that is looking to be freed and benefit from this then you know you need to look past that, as the goal of waking up is to get past the self! Using the optical illusion is a good way to see this. At first, you know there are two perspectives to be seen in the picture, and you are motivated by your ego to "figure it out" and gain status. What happens once you see it is some internal dialogue that says, "Oh boy, I see it!" Something else also happens—in the silence there is a recognition and an understanding. The recognition happens before and beyond thought and dialogue. Pay attention to the silence and to the feeling that accompanies the silent understanding, as this is different than the self that is collecting points for what it claims is "its" accomplishment.

The quicker you can let go of the doer the better. Life does itself. Stop claiming ownership and labeling things as you "being the doer" of them. How much do you really "do"? Research shows that the brain moves the body way before the brain talks about it and says there is a "self" that just did it. Since this is the case, telling yourself that you are the originator of doing and thinking is irrelevant. This is no cause

The Path to Personal Power

for alarm, as life does you and does itself without any need for your agreement, labeling or assistance.

This idea is worth repeating because it assists in letting go. Take solace in the fact that what you are trying to experience is what is actually *so* before you alter it with the habitual overlay your mind creates. It has always been that way—you have just been trained to see it differently. You may have had an experience lying in bed and looking in the near dark at something, maybe a piece of clothing, and for a moment it appears to be an animal. You are jolted a little, your nerves prick up and your anxiety rises. For a moment there is an animal in your bedroom! Then your brain and eyes pick up a different shape, some stripes—and then it is a shirt again. It was always a shirt, but for a moment you were tricked into seeing an animal. For your whole lifetime you have been seeing reality as an animal, and agreeing with others on this as well, and you are looking to experience the shirt underneath your assumptions. The animal you "thought" you saw does not magically transform, although when you see the shirt, something in **you** transforms. Your mind does not "bring about" the shirt-ness from the animal, it lets go of the animal-ness through silence and your practice and re-learns shirt.

At some point you need to realize that NO words really help after a certain point. You learn that they come after the fact. They simply point like a street sign and are not the thing-in-itself. The sign is not the street. Any words that attempt to describe waking up fall short of it. They are always behind the moment and after the fact. The map can never be as detailed as the actual territory. Stay in the present moment, stay in the territory and use the signs to remind you and point you back to the territory and your present moment awareness and practice.

Tying It All Together

Chapter 38
Tying It All Together

After reading the last section, *Waking Up*, and especially after successfully working the methods, you may begin to think and feel that the goals you aspired to when starting the book have taken on a different flavor. This is a good sign, because as you travel down the path and do the work you should not expect to be the same person who started the journey.

Often the initial goal is to add a little horsepower to the person you started as and simply get more done, succeed more and suffer less. Certainly that is a worthwhile motivation and direction, although not the most comprehensive one.

At first the idea of *more* serves to glorify the self as *ego*. After awakening, the embracing of *more* is inherent in serving our true nature and deepening our understanding of it. The idea of *more* is both a noble direction and a risk. *More* can be extremely self-centered and shallow. Consider money and fame, two traps that lure those needing to boost their self-esteem and prop up deep fears of being worthless. More money and fame often end up being sirens that lure people to their demise.

This is why I strongly encourage you to **not** use goals and destinations in life to fix things about yourself that aren't broken—to fix metaphysical value. Just because you aren't famous doesn't mean you aren't worthwhile. Just because you didn't get more than two likes on your last social media post doesn't mean you aren't likable. Technology and marketing have reduced a sensitive generation to a bunch of mice in a maze, repeatedly pushing on a lever to get a reward—a couple of drops of ego boost. The lyrics of "Satisfaction" by the Rolling Stones come to mind:

> When I'm watchin' my TV
> And a man comes on and tells me
> How white my shirts can be

> But he can't be a man 'cause he doesn't smoke
> The same cigarettes as me

I think that Mick Jagger was right to be pissed about the endless barrage of advertising telling us about all our "lacks" and providing salvation for it. Of course *we* vow to ourselves that we will never fall for this—while at the same time *knowing* our life would be just right if we could only get a nicer car. Then all would be well. What I find fascinating is that few people actually look at this pattern of acquisition to see if it works to solve their feeling of lack.

I have not once found the pattern of the acquisition of *more* to fix the problem of metaphysical value—to fix the problem of "I'm not good enough." All it does is shield yourself from shame just a little bit for a little while. It makes you a person who is not good enough, but now has a designer handbag, a luxury car and a stylish haircut. The inner justification will then be "but it's better than being not-good-enough without these things! At least I have these things to cling to!" Personally I do not find this a good enough excuse—or an existence—when looked at in the light of what we are capable of. Not even close.

When you take metaphysical value out of the equation, the drive to fix "I'm not good *enough*" changes. The perspective shifts to your not being good *enough* **at a specific task or skill**—the improvement of which has a pragmatic value and/or purely brings about personal joy and satisfaction. At this point you can decide at what point that task or skill becomes *good-enough*. Good enough to garner a favorable result to an acceptable level of probability that you yourself set based on that task or skill's level of importance to *you*. You can grow a beautiful garden without seeking to win an award for it. You can also grow flowers and enter them into competition. If these goals are separate from your ego and identity, then where you decide is enough is good enough.

At some point your entire matrix of tasks and skills can be taken into account. Based on your priorities and considering the return on investment for your time and energy—your entire life can reach *good-enough*. At this point you can take the leap of faith and, if you have acquired enough personal power, self-define your life and your *self* as GOOD ENOUGH.

The concept of good-enough becomes the antidote for not-good-enough when *you* say it does. When you have cancelled out the drive to fix being not-good-enough, you will need to find different motivation, or more accurately, get reconnected to healthy motivations. These are things like curiosity, playfulness, joy, passion and love. These may seem light and fluffy at first glance, and if that is the case for you, I'd like you to seriously and deeply ponder the following: What else do you think is left when you wipe the slate clean of fear and angst? Are these things not what you are expecting as you near your original undisturbed nature?

The inner drive shifts from "I have to have more" to "I get to have more, I get to do more and I get to give more." You move from compulsion to freedom. Freedom is not necessarily what everyone wants, regardless of what they say. This is because one begins to become free of the need for *identity*. Without the game of fixing what is not-good-enough, you are no longer distracted from some very big questions like "What am I?" and "What is the purpose of all of this?" The *Waking Up* component of the work is essential at this point.

Do Both at the Same Time

I deliberately laid out the book with the *Waking Up* section at the end because this is the way most people progress through the work. My experience is that while many people are interested in waking up, many use the search for awakening to skirt having to grow up and live life. If you try to avoid the "common things," you are taking away the proving ground for your actual aim and thus miss altogether. You cannot wake up into a non-reality because you don't like reality itself.

There are a few people who come to awakening straight on. There are also some to whom it seems to "happen to" more than being brought on by their own efforts. These are not common instances and it is difficult to extrapolate their experience into work that the average person can take up.

I suggest that you pursue the *work* as follows: Re-read the first parts of the book and the *Waking Up* section simultaneously and side-by-side going forward as you DO the DOing as laid out in both parts. As I said at the end of Chapter 2 "Walk through life with a foot in each world…unapologetically." The worlds support and inform each other, and thus, by doing both you get a multiplier effect. There will be times when your progress is enhanced by skewing your focus and, by all means, strike when the iron is hot.

What at first seems like two different worlds becomes one as you progress. The deeper your experience of awakening becomes, the less conflict there is between paradoxical concepts. All aspects of life can be tightened up, refined and mastered on the way to deepening your awakening. Although the source and depth of motivation have changed, life continues to provide us with ample opportunities to learn and grow.

Drop the Need for *Feeling* Certainty

Many people that I work with struggle with just being who and where they are. What do I mean by this? They struggle with the fact that they are *not yet who and where they want to be.* They are terrified of the fact that they don't know everything. They want to start out at the top, as a perennial winner, as someone who has all the skills and wisdom—they want to start out as a black belt (at *least* first degree). They think that this is the answer to the problem. What is the problem when you boil everything down? **They are uncomfortable with being *uncomfortable.*** They do not like being a wobbly beginner. They can't stand *not-knowing*. They are insecure about being average, or below average or anything less than outstanding.

Fortunately, being uncomfortable with being uncomfortable is not so hard to fix. First, I suggest you understand what is going on with this pattern and what its function is. My guess is that the feelings of discomfort, or wobble and of not-knowing, are so close to the feelings of shame, loss of status and of being not-good-enough that they seem indistinguishable unless examined very closely. The pattern is 1) have these feelings, 2) avoid the behaviors that cause them, 3) tell yourself you are safe or better off because the feelings dissipate. The function of the pattern is protective—it is self/identity/status/ego preserving.

If this is in fact what is going on (and it often is) then we need to do some reframing. How do we know that the life outcome is the same as the purported function? We don't, and in most cases, it isn't. If the function is safety, self-preservation and maintaining status/ego, then reframe this into "growth-prevention." If we stop learning and growing as individuals, then we can almost guarantee stagnation in the future. We can almost guarantee that other people, especially our competitors, will surpass us. So, in essence, this is a self-diminishing behavior in the long run. It may *seem* to be self-enhancing in the short term because fears dissipate. These fearful feelings lie to us and deceive us into "believing" that their presence equals risk of self-diminishment and their absence equals safety and self-enhancement. The new understanding is that the feelings prevent us from becoming who we want to be and going where we want to go. If you take it a step further, it could be that these feelings of fear mean you are learning and on your way to success!

If you know that you hate the feeling of fear, and that some fear and uncertainty is the way forward to brighter horizons, then you have a choice to make. You can choose to **behave anyway** and get on with the doing you need to do. You can choose to be nice to yourself and set reasonable expectations. You can choose to act when you don't *feel* like it. The following sentiment has been attributed to many different people, although I like this one the best.

> "Courage is being scared to death…and saddling up anyway."
> — John Wayne

You cannot control outcomes as much as you like. You **can put the odds more in your favor.** Your first career may not be your last. Every stock you buy will not go straight up. You may not win your first race or even finish it. But…you cannot win unless you have those "firsts." Putting off doing will not change the fears and wobbles and eventual successes. It will only delay the learning and progress. It may delay it past the point of no return if you are not careful. The clock is running so start *NOW*.

You should not become a sailor expecting calm seas. You should learn to tolerate, then master and enjoy the challenge of sailing on all seas, because that is what makes you a legendary captain. To be a legendary captain of yourself and your life you need to *start* DOing and *keep* DOing.

When you really do the work, you are likely to feel that you are doing something wrong and bad. Your nervous system generates this for you to keep you out of trouble with the "authorities." On the one hand you are excited to create yourself and your life into *your* work of art. On the other hand, you might feel anxious, scared and braced for something bad to happen.

When I was in grade school I was fascinated by the idea of ghosts and demons. One of the scary party games was "light as a feather, stiff as a board," in which a group tells a person who is lying down about their death, starts chanting "light as a feather, stiff as a board" and then lifts that person off the ground using only two fingers each. I was too scared to try it.

My personal favorite legend went along the lines of filling up a bathtub, turning off the lights, lighting a candle and then doing some chanting and spells at midnight to summon a demon woman who would rise up out of the water. For years after hearing this story, every time I was in a bathroom at nighttime and saw the bathtub I got spooked. I would move out of bathrooms *quickly* after turning off the lights. After a while I got tired of being scared and powerless against the dark forces. So one night, instead of turning off the bathroom light and hightailing it out of there, I decided to turn off the light, turn around, tear back the shower curtain and say "Come and get me you bitch! If there are demons in this universe, I dare you to come and get me, you pussies!" As far as I've been able to figure out, these entities must like me because they haven't come to get me yet. (I say this tongue-in-cheek and have to include this sentence for fear that people will contact me to ask me about my positive working relationship with evil spirits...although it *is* positive.)

Think back over all the ground we've covered. Recall the reason you started reading this book and what you hoped you might accomplish for yourself. Think about all of your hopes and dreams and especially of all the fears we've been looking at. Let the demons come for you. Tempt the fates. Touch the electric fence again...see for yourself if it has been turned off. Perhaps it was never *really* there. See if you get struck by lightning, spontaneously combust or are swallowed by the earth for being who you are and making that into the special work of art it can be. Fuck it. What do you really have to lose?

> **Bonus Great Secret**
> There is very little to lose that isn't in the story about what you are afraid to lose!

Let it go.

About the Author

Cal Iwema has worked in the field of psychology and applied philosophy for over 20 years as a psychotherapist and executive coach. He was a long-time student of Dr. Christopher S. Hyatt and contributing author.

His interests include playing guitar, electronic music, craft cocktails, wine, woodworking, art, motorcycles, shooting, family and friends, and his German shepherd, Zen.

He will occasionally work with individuals on the material presented in his books. Inquire at his website:

www.bestmindforward.com

FROM CALVIN IWEMA, M.A.

ENERGIZED HYPNOSIS
A Non-Book for Self-Change
With Christopher S. Hyatt, Ph.D.

Energized Hypnosis is a **breakthrough** program of videos, audios, booklets and a "non-book" for gaining personal power, peace of mind and enlightenment. The techniques of **Energized Hypnosis** were developed many years ago by Dr. Christopher Hyatt and Dr. Israel Regardie, but have remained "in the closet"...until now.

THE BIG BLACK BOOK
Christopher S. Hyatt, Ph.D. & Friends

Most sections of *The Big Black Book* were written by Christopher S. Hyatt along with his friends and colleagues between 2003 and 2008 and were originally published as individual booklets. Now the entire series has been collected into this single volume. But what is *The Big Black Book* about?

Little more can be said lest we give away its intent and reduce its impact.

THE *Original* FALCON PRESS

Invites You to Visit Our Website:
http://originalfalcon.com

At our website you can:

- Browse the online catalog of all of our great titles
- Find out what's available and what's out of stock
- Get special discounts
- Order our titles through our secure online server
- Find products not available anywhere else including:
    - One of a kind and limited availability products
    - Special packages
    - Special pricing
- Get free gifts
- Join our email list for advance notice of New Releases and Special Offers
- Find out about book signings and author events
- Send email to our authors
- Read excerpts of many of our titles
- Find links to our authors' websites
- Discover links to other weird and wonderful sites
- And much, much more

Get online today at http://originalfalcon.com

www.ingramcontent.com/pod-product-compliance
Lightning Source LLC
LaVergne TN
LVHW021709060526
838200LV00050B/2581